THE
SACRED SCIENCE
OF
ANCIENT JAPAN

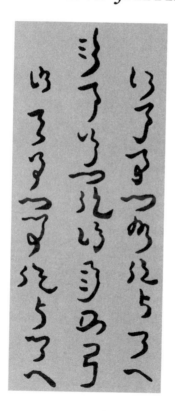

THE SACRED SCIENCE OF ANCIENT JAPAN

Lost Chronicles of the Age of the Gods

AVERY MORROW

Bear & Company
Rochester, Vermont • Toronto, Canada

Bear & Company
One Park Street
Rochester, Vermont 05767
www.BearandCompanyBooks.com

Text stock is SFI certified

Library of Congress Cataloging-in-Publication Data
Morrow, Avery, 1987–
  The sacred science of ancient Japan : lost chronicles of the age of the gods / Avery
Morrow.
      pages cm
  Includes bibliographical references and index.
  Summary: "The first English translation and examination of secret Japanese
writings dating from the paleolithic to classical eras"—Provided by publisher.
  ISBN 978-1-59143-170-1 (pbk.) — ISBN 978-1-59143-750-5 (e-book)
  1. Japan—History—To 645. 2. Mythology, Japanese. I. Title.
  DS855.M678 2014
  952'.01—dc23
                                                              2013015197

Printed and bound in the United States by Lake Book Manufacturing, Inc.
The text stock is SFI certified. The Sustainable Forestry Initiative® program
promotes sustainable forest management.

10   9   8   7   6   5   4   3   2   1

Text design and layout by Virginia Scott Bowman
This book was typeset in Garamond Premier Pro and Gill Sans with Centaur and
Gill Sans used as display typefaces

To send correspondence to the author of this book, mail a first-class letter to the
author c/o Inner Traditions • Bear & Company, One Park Street, Rochester, VT
05767, and we will forward the communication, or contact the author directly at
avery.morrow.name/chokodai.

For my parents

Contents

Acknowledgments

When I began researching this subject, I had little understanding of its true importance. I was reading and writing out of pure curiosity, and nothing I had learned in my childhood or education could have let me in on the secret of the deep, perennial symbolism that these unusual documents convey. The book you are now holding exists because a close friend of mine unlocked the gate for me and turned my idle studies into something worth thinking about. It was E. S. B. who gave my research meaning, and it was E. S. B. who corrected my errors and showed me the way to the Grail. If this book turns out to be meaningful to anyone, it is E. S. B. whom you should thank.

I corresponded with a number of people who provided extra background information for this book. Professor John Bentley of Northern Illinois University answered my questions about the *Sendai Kuji Hongi,* and Matt Treyvaud offered some comments on the Hifumi Song. Shin'ichi Nakaya assisted me in the description of the *Hitsuki Shinji.* Permission to reproduce Andrew Driver's translations of the *Hotsuma Tsutaye* was graciously provided by Hotsumatsutae Japan, a project of the Japan Translation Center at http://www.hotsuma.gr.jp. Yoko Inada provided me with her late husband's rare work on the Katakamuna Documents. Minoru Harada, a very resourceful guy, answered my questions on Twitter. Finally, Masafumi Kume wrote a marvelous book about Katsutoki Sakai and generously invited me to an interview with the custodian of the Takenouchi Documents. All the people I have listed just now are experts, and if they read this book expecting a similarly expert opinion, I can only offer my apologies.

Many hands helped bring this text to publication. I would like to thank the esoterica professor who introduced me to Bear & Company and the editors known and unknown to me who approved my submission, cleaned up my manuscript, and made this book possible. Their hard work has paid off by making a much more interesting book available to a much wider audience. I am grateful that Inner Traditions/Bear & Company brings unique and meaningful books to press every year, and I am overwhelmed to be included among these ranks.

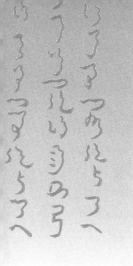

INTRODUCTION

A Romance in
a Fog

In Japan a large number of books claiming to be the true and ancient origin story of the nation have appeared since the seventeenth century. The authenticity of these documents is thrown into doubt by the scanty evidence for their premodern existence, their occasional anachronisms, and their primordial writing systems that are largely unattested in the historical record. They are pushed to the margins of acceptable discourse, literally hidden under the UFO and New Age shelves at some bookstores. Despite rejection by the establishment they continue to garner amateur proponents around the country who investigate the possibility that they might tell us something about the ultra-ancient world.

The worlds described in these texts do not resemble our modern, archeological idea of the ancient world, nor is it the Stone Age of the popular imagination. Instead, these texts seem to offer tantalizing fragments of a different kind of knowledge. It is the kind of science Dante refers to in the *Inferno* when he says, "Go back to your science, which teaches that the more a creature is perfect, the more it perceives the good, and likewise pain." Today's writers call this form of knowledge "sacred science," and the setting in which we will learn this science is an incalculably ancient Japan.

For convenience I will refer to these documents as *parahistories*

1

and the readings and studies that derive from them as *parahistorical*.* Their contents are as diverse as real ancient documents, and the reasons for studying them are just as unpredictable. One researcher may be interested in understanding the primal sounds of ultra-ancient Japanese, while another may be trying to understand what kind of festivals were celebrated in ultra-ancient Japan. Working whenever they can find the time they slowly decipher ancient languages and unknown scripts, fitting together a great puzzle, the pieces of which are scattered across the modern nation in distant mountains and forgotten shrines.

This book focuses on four of these texts. There are many more with equally complex stories, but these four strike me as having particular values that deserve commentary and a close reading, not only for their similarities, but for their extreme differences.

The *Sendai Kuji Hongi Taiseikyō* (allegedly written in 620 CE, appearing in 1679), also known as the *Kujiki-72*, offers ancient knowledge discovered by the Classical Age genius Prince Shōtoku. It claims to be the full version of Shōtoku's long-lost history of Japan, conveying not only the real, unbiased story of the high ancient lords, but also an intricate plan for a good society balancing politics and religion and including prophecies, laws, and music.

The *Hotsuma Tsutaye* (allegedly written in 100 CE, appearing in 1775) purports to be the record of a forgotten ancient civilization in Japan written in a sacred indigenous script. A 10,000-line epic poem in an unfamiliar language that resembles ancient Japanese, it presents Japan's gods and kings of the Heroic Age as real individuals, and its worldview seems to parallel the esoteric teachings of medieval Buddhist sects.

---

*The Japanese word for parahistory is *koshi-koden* 古史古伝, four Chinese characters, which together mean something like "old histories and old legends." Although my coined word loses a bit of apparent neutrality, in practice there is the same understanding that koshi-koden challenges standard history.

The Takenouchi Documents (allegedly written in prehistory, appearing in 1921) go beyond the Heroic Age into the deep and forbidden history of the Golden Age. Written in hundreds of different ancient scripts, they place the origins of all the great religions of the world into one single Tradition preserved in Japan. Oddly, the Tradition they describe has parallels in certain Western doctrines that were only then coming to light.

The Katakamuna Documents (allegedly written in prehistory, appearing in 1966) make almost no pretense at being the sort of history taught in textbooks. Rather, they are an entirely esoteric text with parahistorical songs acting as the medium of choice to convey a powerful holistic knowledge of incalculable, even perennial, age.

A proper understanding of the message of these unusual and exciting documents requires knowledge of the ancient history and legends they emerge from and the esoteric concepts they employ. To begin with let's learn how history is told in Japan, and why this makes the nation uniquely suited to inherit parahistories.

JAPAN AND THE DECLINE OF THE GENERATIONS

The officially acknowledged history of the Japanese nation begins with its earliest surviving documents, the *Kojiki* and the *Nihon Shoki*. These two classical texts are the most important source for the lives of the early emperors and key events in the formation of Japan, and to some extent they imitate the model of earlier Chinese annals, which focused on the reigns of emperors and kings. But unlike the Chinese histories they also incorporate oral traditions of the unknowable eons stretching from the beginning of the universe to the mists of prehistory. In Japan the origin of the universe and the creation of the first humans is part of the traditional narrative of history and becomes in effect a historical question, rather than a scientific, political, or religious one.

Needless to say, very few people in Japan today actually believe that these two documents describe the real creation of the world or the origin of the Japanese people. Scientific archaeology has shown that before the imperial court Japan had a long primitive era when people used stone tools, called the Jōmon period, and an iron age where people developed social structure, refined clothing, and built large wooden structures, called the Yayoi period.

But conflict with the *Kojiki* and *Nihon Shoki* cannot be avoided. A rationally minded reader would expect those documents to retain some memory of earlier, less civilized eras. In fact, against such expectations, the *opposite* is true. These ancient histories do not give an impression of rising up out of primitiveness. Instead, human beings are descended directly from the gods! In both books the gods create the islands of Japan, fight and love there, and give birth to the first humans who then begin the imperial institution by divine right. Even after the focus of the histories switches to the material world, interactions between men and gods remain constant throughout the narrative.

These legends of a spiritual past of immense power are not limited to Japan but can be found everywhere that primeval texts have survived into the present. The Greek poet Hesiod tells us of Four Ages of humanity, but rather than being a story of four stages of ascent from darkness into light, they speak of a descent from immortal, immaterial spiritual bodies into weak physical forms. The Vedas of India have a very similar narrative, as do the Mayan world cycles. Even the Bible has this basic story of a fall from grace, and Jewish tradition speaks of the decline of the generations, the *yeridat ha-dorot*. The consistency of these stories from around the world is familiar to many of us, but we very rarely ask the probing question: Why did so many different cultures, in their own earliest writings, contradict what we would believe to be a fact within their historical memory?

These origin stories, and the ancient messages they carry to the present, are easily downplayed by scientific examinations of human origins but cannot be lost. Just as the Old Testament continues to hold weight throughout the Western world and is the basis of many people's beliefs in one way or another, the autochthonic Japanese origin story can never truly be scrubbed from cultural memory and continues to be an object of fascination for hundreds of thousands, if not millions, of people throughout the country. There is an undying thirst for books about the enigmatic ancient myths and the equally mysterious Chinese reports of a kingdom called Yamatai and a queen named Himiko.

THE MENACE AND
PROMISE OF HISTORIOGRAPHY

Obviously the texts I will soon discuss do not carry the standard power of an origin story because they are not standard history. To call them authentic is a heresy before the state and the academy. These authorities have either ignored the parahistories or have actively conspired to suppress them. Modern researchers present them to the public as secret history concealed by these groups. But they cannot be dubbed folklore because they have never been part of the popular culture. Since they can basically be considered fringe, alternative history, what value do these texts have to Japan and the world at large?

To answer this question I will look to the work of the twentieth-century Italian philosopher and mountaineer Julius Evola and his spiritual antecedent, the French metaphysician René Guénon. Evola once purposefully composed a sort of parahistory, prefacing it with the bold claim that any history told by anyone merely reflects the needs of the current age, and regardless of the amount of verification provided, *truth* is metaphysical and lies beyond evidence.

A few examples of this will make clear what Evola was talking about. From the 1820s to roughly the 1960s the Founding Fathers were revered in America as brilliant minds, and children were taught to follow the examples of Washington and Jefferson. Washington was famously said to have never told a lie. An Italian-American painted "The Apotheosis of Washington" on the ceiling of the Capitol showing the first president ascending to godhood. Today this reverence makes some Americans cringe, and revisionists are constantly reminding us that the Founding Fathers were mean to people sometimes and many of them kept slaves. Both of these modes of thought reflect the needs of their respective eras. Neither of them is *the* correct history. Different stories are told to children in order to acquaint them with the attitude society expects them to adopt toward the past.

Another familiar example is that of Marx's attempt to control history. As Hannah Arendt notes in her essay "Tradition and the Modern Age," Marx does not open *The Communist Manifesto* with a claim about society or humanity, but about history: "The history of all hitherto existing society is the history of class struggles." If Marx can persuade the reader to accept this historical narrative, then the establishment of Communism itself will become a historical inevitability in the reader's mind, and the only choice remaining is whether to side with the progressive future or with the regressive past. To realize that the narrative itself might be flawed, one must look outside Marx and Marxist historians.

Returning to the subject of origin stories, in these matters the metaphysics behind a story takes on epic levels of drama and weight. The story of mankind progressing from primate and caveman states to early, inferior kingdoms and modern, democratic splendor is a myth made to fit the present era. It creates a suitable story for its desired *truth* by identifying "mankind" with the physical body and scientifically tracing the story of this body back through the centuries. If our metaphysics holds a conflicting claim, if we believe for example that human beings are essentially souls descended into bodies, then the entire story of these bodies is irrelevant to mankind and can be discarded. C. S. Lewis, like many traditional thinkers, has affirmed this view: "We Christians don't call [wisdom] 'evolution' because we believe it isn't something coming up out of blind Nature but something coming down from the world of light and power and knowledge beyond all Nature."

We may also use this rule to understand that material evidence is irrelevant to debates over human origins. Darwinists and Creationists are arguing from different basic assumptions, although in this modern, materialist age, theists often fall into the trap of inventing shoddy scientific evidence for their metaphysical claim. In fact, science is irrelevant to determining which of these stories is right; it is a choice that must be made by the individual observer in accordance with his own beliefs. No matter how much evidence is offered up, you cannot turn the material claim of natural selection into a spiritual claim about the origin of the soul. Evola theorized that our images of ancient civilizations contain spiritual truths greater than any material claims that could be confirmed by historians or archaeologists, as he explains in *Revolt Against the Modern World:*

> Every epoch has its own "myth" through which it reflects a given collective climate. Today the aristocratic idea that mankind has higher origins, namely, a past of light and of spirit, has been replaced by the democratic idea of evolutionism, which derives the higher from the lower, man from animal, civilization from barbarism. This is not so much the "objective" result of a free and conscious scientific inquiry, but rather one of the many reflections that the advent of the modern world, characterized by inferior social and spiritual strata and by man without traditions, has necessarily produced on the intellectual and cultural plane. Thus we should not delude ourselves: some "positive" superstitions will always produce alibis to defend themselves. The acknowledgment of new horizons will be possible not through the discovery of new "findings," but rather through a new attitude toward these findings. Any attempt to validate even from a scientific perspective what the traditional dogmatic point of view upholds will generate results only among those who are already spiritually well disposed to accept this kind of knowledge.[1]

This warning appears in the middle of Evola's book, right before his focus shifts from a discussion of various classical and medieval philosophies to actually writing a narrative of the distant past. In one of the most difficult and obtuse sections of his entire oeuvre, Evola takes us on an epic tour of the human race that begins with the original spiritual home of the Aryan race in Hyperborea (i.e., the Arctic Circle) and links all world cultures to either that land or Atlantis. Readers who were skeptical but able to follow Evola's line of thought up until that point will be lost by the second half of the book if they are not "spiritually well disposed." Facts are no longer giving us insight into the past—now the ultimate story of origin shines its light on the facts.

This is the attitude we must adopt to parahistory: These origin stories are not meant to be digested as scientific reports about material conditions that can be judged for accuracy against archaeological data and interpreted by an alien or a computer, but are rather the start of a narrative of tremendous value to human beings (in this case, the Japanese) and of no importance to anyone else. Indeed, when we examine parahistories as the central pillars of their respective metaphysical frameworks rather than trying to analyze them as produced documents, we happen upon an interesting problem.

The problem is this: Parahistories are no less believable than the mythological portions of the *Kojiki* and *Nihon Shoki*. The only material advantage the two official histories have over the parahistories is that we can be reasonably certain the official histories really are 1,300 years old. Beyond that, Japan's position is uniquely open to rewriting the past. Certainly it is bizarre to say that Moses flew to Japan and studied imperial doctrine. But is it not equally bizarre to say that Japan was created, and at one time inhabited, by powerful divinities?

We believe, like Evola, that the power of parahistories lies in the fact that they are *not* fiction but possess a "well disposed" readership that sees them as a real and secret history. The ancient languages they were written in demonstrate to modern readers that one who wants to be truly knowledgeable about these documents must first be initiated into the mysterious world of ancient Japan. Analysis as literature would neglect the value they have to these proponents. Even if they are completely unbelievable to outsiders, the ambiguity caused by the claim of historicity places them in a different genre of writing.

What Kind of World Will We See?

In one of Jorge Luis Borges's most famous stories, "Tlön, Uqbar, Orbis Tertius," Borges and his friends become obsessed with unraveling a mystery about the fictional planet of Tlön and the language and literature that its authors have invented. The culture of Tlön is foreign and alien to theirs, and its imaginary language is that of a strange alien species, but as their obsession grows Earth begins to resemble Tlön. Is this sort of weird tale the kind of world parahistory imagines?

This is what I thought at first, but the parahistorians themselves proved me wrong. Even though Japan may be a strange land to many of my readers, and although these texts are clearly quite unusual even for Japanese people, these documents are not *attempting* to be weird but are rather aiming to transmit a message from what Evola calls "an invisible and intangible dimension that is the support, the source, and the true life" above and beyond our mortal existence.[2] Are they successful? I will let you be the judge.

Skeptics of this genre may pursue it as an idle curiosity, but the proponents of these documents state, time and time again, that they are important, they are meaningful, and the world would be changed for the better if more people learned about them. Parahistory is not a subject for an afternoon's entertainment; the future of the world hangs in the balance. If the majority of people knew what was contained in these documents, they say, so much of the uncertainty in our lives could be conquered by the knowledge of our true inheritance. We would have a starting point for mutual understanding of so many different things. If only!

Through parahistory we can perceive a new realm of possibilities. The parahistorians would agree with G. K. Chesterton: "Most possibly we are in Eden still. It is only our eyes that have changed." The ancient Japan of these texts is a possible Eden, and reading parahistories provides a window into it. As we will see, when we look through these windows we will discover compelling memories of many possible pasts, all of them projecting a hopeful message into the present, but with many complexities and difficulties.

Each of the texts summarized in this book has had several full-length commentaries written about it in Japanese. None of the texts are written in standard Japanese, as some use unique writing systems and others use different languages. We could not possibly hope to grasp them completely in a single chapter. Instead, I will showcase some of the most intriguing and praiseworthy elements of each of the texts, and then I will explain the context in which they are studied by their adherents with the aim of showing that they are worthy of closer investigation from those willing to take the time to study and learn.

Just as you are hopefully reading this book with good faith today, so you should read the works of ancient and medieval writers with good faith, trying to understand what they are pointing toward and why it is important for you as much as them. It is often hard to unravel the mysteries and figure out what, exactly, they were talking about, but therein lies the great puzzle of parahistory. The researcher Kōji Imura provides a reflection on the adventure that lies within:

> It is impossible to believe that all the "traditions" bequeathed to us in the parahistories are equally true, because their contents are replete with forgeries and falsifications. However, it goes without saying that this misgiving does not limit itself to parahistory, but extends to the *Kojiki* and *Nihon Shoki* as well. Also, as modern parapsychology has made clear, behaviors like hearsay, folklore, and recitation will naturally create errors through transmission, and as the centuries pass, the corruption or alteration of oral traditions can also be said to be natural.
>
> Seen from this perspective, we may make sense of the disputes over parahistory which are often difficult to parse. What's more, a person who has managed to work his way into this field cannot easily leave it behind, for he will come to enjoy the fulfilling journeys which let him sense a mysterious allure and romance in a fog.[3]

Parahistory is very much a romance in a fog. Each document has its strangely familiar passages that bewitch one's mind with inexplicable ancient images, making it difficult to abandon the subject as Imura says, but to achieve these moments one must wade through a thicket of ancient history, language, legend, and contradictions with accepted history. Moreover, when we translate the texts into English, something indescribable about the original context and magic about the work is lost. I will strive to balance the necessary background to understand the work with some choice passages and summaries to excite the imagination.

How to Pronounce Japanese

The Japanese language is very easy to pronounce. There are no silent letters, and there are no plurals or declensions. All vowels are pronounced the same way:

> A as in "father"
>
> I as in "ink"
>
> U as in "blue"
>
> E as in "end"
>
> O as in "low"

For example, the name *Amaterasu* is pronounced Ah-Mah-Teh-Rah-Sue and *Hitsuki* is pronounced Hee-Tsoo-Kee. Sometimes an "N" will stand on its own, for example, *Nihonjin,* Knee-Hone-Jean.

Long marks over vowels mean their sounds are more drawn out, so "Shōtoku" will be pronounced Show-Oh-Toe-Koo, as opposed to Sho'-Toe-Koo. These are included for painstaking accuracy, but if you don't understand them, don't punish yourself trying to reproduce them.

Reading Japanese text in the original script is much more difficult than pronouncing it, but you will not be asked to read Japanese at any point in this book.

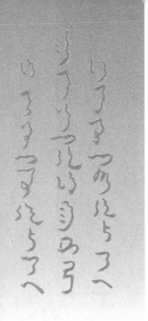

1
Passport
to Parahistory

Ancient Japan's Mysteries

What kind of nation is Japan, and who are the Japanese? When Japanese people ask themselves this, their first inclination is often to go back to the earliest sources. Today we have a wide variety of texts and archaeological evidence to tell us how Japan came together as a nation and what important events happened in its earliest days. Yet these official sources are somehow unfulfilling. Unlike the founding myths of Rome or the American Constitution, they do not quickly answer questions about what kind of country has been founded on the Japanese archipelago. It is with good reason that the great parahistorian Katsutoki Sakai said, "the more we think, the more we realize that Japanese high ancient history is a great puzzle."[1]

The following chapters explore unusual, strange, and exciting historical texts. Most explorers are aware that how you pack your bag before setting out on a journey is of paramount importance. Building up a little background knowledge is absolutely essential for understanding these parahistories. These documents are full of all sorts of obscure allusions and parallels, and there is no time in this sightseeing expedition to hunt all of them down. Instead, I will cover only the most essential facts that all prospective parahistorians should know, doing so in a general order from fairly standard schoolbook knowledge to obscure trivia for history buffs only.

FOUR SOURCES OF ANCIENT JAPAN

Archaeology provides us with the most certain account of how Japanese people lived in the past, although we can only guess why artifacts were made or what they mean. The evidence, for what it is, shows that Japan had an ordinary Paleolithic era tens of thousands of years ago, followed by the Jōmon period during which the ancestors of the Japanese produced beautiful, immediately recognizable pottery and clay humanoid figures known as *dogū* (fig. 1.1). The elaborate dogū figurines, which some claim resemble astronauts, are well known but do not factor into the parahistories. The Jōmon period, which is not characterized by anything more complex than clay work and music, ended in 300 BCE. Today, popular stories and comic books depict the Jōmon people living a simple hunter-gatherer lifestyle similar to their Far Eastern neighbors.

Following the Jōmon people were the Yayoi. In the final centuries before Christ, people fleeing violence in East Asia immigrated to Japan and mixed freely with the local population, creating an entirely new culture unlike the Jōmon or anything in Asia. Archaeologists have found the remains of great chiefdoms from the Yayoi period that produced a large number of elaborate mirrors, swords, and a type of curved jade bead called *magatama*. These three unique products of the Yayoi, not coincidentally, are the same objects held sacred in Japan as the Three Treasures of the Emperor, which have been handed down in the imperial family for thousands of years. While only the Emperor and ritual officials are allowed access to the Three Treasures today, medieval descriptions confirm that they are one and the same with the characteristic Yayoi products that archaeologists have discovered. The Yayoi also created bronze bells, cultivated rice, and organized themselves into large towns, one of which has been carefully recreated in Yoshinogari Town in Saga prefecture.

Figure 1.1. A dogū figurine at the Tokyo National Museum.

The Chinese *Chronicle of the Wei* dating to 280 CE is the first description of Japan acknowledged by modern academic historians. This protohistory was downplayed before 1868 because the *Nihon Shoki* and

Kojiki were considered standard, but in the imperial period it became an essential part of understanding ancient Japan. Today its enigmatic description of a third-century Japanese kingdom called Yamatai and its priestess-queen Himiko have caught the popular imagination, and it is difficult to walk into a bookstore in Japan without finding Yamatai or Himiko mentioned somewhere. The standard Japanese image of a Yayoi period man or woman—dressed in white, with loops in their hair, wearing a necklace made of beads and magatama—is derived from the descriptions in this chronicle, supplemented by archaeology. The location of Yamatai, however, has proven elusive and the chronicle contains some fantastic elements.

The Yamatai record gets some of its charm from Himiko's name, which sounds a bit like "princess girl," and the idea that Japan's tribes were once unified under a female ruler who served as both queen and high priestess. Images of a spunky warrior girl in priestly Yayoi period robes, sometimes sporting a magatama necklace or a mirror, are widespread in Japan and always bring a smile to my face when I see them. For example, a short comic by the famous artist Kamui Fujiwara depicts young Himiko struggling with tribal politics and bringing together a nation with her spiritual vision of the future, which seems to lead right up to the twentieth century. Unfortunately, the real Himiko is clearly described in the chronicle as being an old woman.

After the Chinese account there is a long silence in the historical record, after which the Yayoi period in archaeology becomes the Kofun period where the tombs of the emperors are made from great mounds of earth. These *kofun*, "old mounds," can still be found scattered across Japan today. Parahistories aside, Japan produced its first acknowledged writings during the Asuka period from 538 to 710 CE, but only very short sentences and inscriptions from these survive today. In this era Japan was strongly influenced by Buddhism and foreign immigration. This was also the era of Prince Shōtoku whose wisdom will be described in the next chapter.

Finally in the early eighth century, called the Heian period, the first extant Japanese chronicles appear, but they create more questions than answers. One of the chronicles, the *Nihon Shoki* (*Chronicle of Japan*), is a history text written in Classical Chinese in a close imitation of Chinese historical style that sometimes even copies phrases directly from Chinese histories. It discusses the history of Japan from the beginning of the world to the noble deeds of the emperors. In medieval Japan the *Nihon Shoki* was the standard history of the beginning of time to 697 CE and was followed by five sequels that extended it to 887 CE. These six standard histories list many different variants that contradict each other in interesting ways. Medieval and early modern commentators often argued over which of the *Nihon Shoki* texts told the real story.

In the eighteenth century an ambitious historian named Norinaga Motoori cast aside the debates over the different *Nihon Shoki* variants entirely and turned his attention to another book called the *Kojiki* (*Records of Old*), which basically only has one variant, but which is written in an impenetrable orthographic pidgin of Japanese and Chinese. The *Kojiki* claims it was written just eight years before the *Nihon Shoki*. It covers the same ground and tells many of the same stories, but lacks its clarity and classical flourishes. Medieval historians believed it to be a useless forgery, but since Motoori the *Kojiki* has been reevaluated as Japan's true earliest text. Motoori sparked a revolution in Japanese historiography that reasserted the importance of the Emperor and eventually became the foundation for the 1868 Meiji Restoration, causing Japan to transform from a secluded island into a powerful modern empire. Parahistorians do not fail to see the moral of this story: A history that was once discarded can after many centuries become official and honored, with endless possibilities for transforming and renewing the spirit of the nation.

But Motoori also opened the door to many questions. If we assume the *Nihon Shoki* was written in 720 and the *Kojiki* in 712, as most historians do today, it is hard to know what to think. Why were two different national histories written in such a short space of time? Why doesn't the *Nihon Shoki* quote or acknowledge the existence of the *Kojiki*, as the *Kojiki* acknowledges its own sources? Some have proposed a political explanation, but there are no significant political differences between the two. Actually, the major differences between the two books are enigmatic and do not suggest any clear reason for revision.

The well-written *Nihon Shoki* is said to be bolstering the imperial house's claim to authority, but at the same time it contains several variants of different stories, explicitly acknowledging a lack of certainty over history. Meanwhile, the single narrative of the *Kojiki* is stylistically messier and hard to read and is not fit to show off to Japan's neighbors. Close examination of government documents shows that even as these histories were being prepared around 700 CE, other, older texts were being abandoned or destroyed. As we will learn in the next chapter, yet another history called the *Kujiki,* with unusual, unique information, may have been written at this same time and then left unfinished.

Even the provenance of these histories is, as Sakai said, quite puzzling. It seems that the process of producing Japan's earliest extant histories involved many behind-the-scenes revisions for reasons unclear to us today. This alone gives parahistorians good cause to doubt the accuracy of the official story. When we start to investigate the stories that these histories tell, we find many more puzzles to be solved.

WHO ARE THE KAMI?

The authors of the earliest Japanese literature found the country simply a lovely place to live and referred to it as *mahoroba*—the "splendid land among the nations." From those earliest eras they recognized that the subtle grandeur of the land is tied intimately to the fact that it was once the home of beings called kami. The word kami, best translated as *Lord,* can also be rendered as god in the Greek sense. The teachings of the *Kojiki* and *Nihon Shoki* mention a great many kami and a number of legends about them, but most of the time the behavior of the kami is obscure or even inexplicable. In the Middle Ages it became common to say that "the ways of the kami are a difficult thing to speculate about." The meaning of the word "kami" has been a source of intense debate for centuries. In the parahistories it takes on various meanings, from referring to great heroes of the past, to a sort of Greek pantheon living outside our physical world, to a single, cosmic spirit. Kami create the world, but also inhabit it. Perhaps the ancient Japanese agreed with the ancient Greeks that "a man is a mortal god, and a god is an immortal man."[2] But in the official histories, kami die from injuries, and are brought back to life by other kami. Maybe, as some Japanese writers have suggested, kami are simply beings with pure hearts, but the motives of the kami in the official histories sometimes appear to be less than pure. Because we should keep these ambiguities in mind, in this book we will mostly keep the word kami untranslated.

A Happy Ambiguity

For most Japanese people it is sufficient to know that kami are figures who lived in the past. On their continued existence in the present day the jury is still out, except for the small matter that they continue to be enshrined in the landscape (fig 1.2). There are over 100,000 shrines to kami throughout Japan, often called *Shinto shrines* in Western literature, but we must understand this as a generalization. Because Japanese does not distinguish plurals from singulars, it is helpful to translate Shinto as "ways of the kami," reminding us that there are multiple ways and multiple understandings of kami, so shrines don't try to control people's freedom to believe or disbelieve.

Calling something a shrine means only that kami are involved. A shrine may be affiliated with an organization, or it may be independent of any group or part of a private household or may even be a business. The kami memorialized in the shrine may be from the official histories or a notable person who died in the area or even a completely unknown name. Some shrines want to promote the belief that visiting and purchasing services can lead to a happy relationship, an easy childbirth, or success in life, but Japanese people do not assume that visiting a shrine implies endorsement of any particular doctrine. The shrinekeeper's belief about the shrine is his private opinion and is never foisted on visitors. Visiting a shrine does not mean you believe that the kami has control over you, any more than visiting the White House makes you an American.

Figure 1.2. Kazahinomi-no-miya, a major shrine at Ise Jingū.

Consider the case of Halloween in America. Most Americans are clueless as to the holiday's origin, but everyone knows how to respond to a trick-or-treater on Halloween. Every household is expected to participate, but there is no punishment for those who don't. The biggest fear is of taking food from potentially dangerous strangers in your neighborhood, but in reality the neighborhood gets to know each other and grows closer together. Local areas in Japan are full of festivals like this, celebrated simply because they are fun and have been carried on for a long time. Shrines are where the implements for these festivals are kept, and most Japanese people do not visit them regularly, only for holidays and special occasions. They serve as neighborhood historical sites and are not seen as "the Japanese religion" except by a small minority. Even shrinekeepers often consider themselves to be nonreligious.

The single most popular day to visit a shrine is New Year's Day, when families come together for a few days and renew their bonds for the new year. When you enter a shrine the custom is to wash your hands and gargle some water, a ritual meant to imply entering with a pure heart. Popular things to do at shrines include getting your fortune told, purchasing good luck charms, praying to or honoring the kami, and sometimes enjoying a flea market or a festival.

Those searching for idols will do so in vain, for there are no depictions of the kami at a shrine. Usually only a small, round mirror is placed inside the building. Ordinary Japanese people visiting a shrine might not know who is enshrined there, even at the major facilities. For some people the question of whom they are bowing to might even be less relevant than the architecture of the building. All this concurs precisely with Julius Evola, who wrote, "One would look in vain for 'religion' in the original forms of the world of Tradition. There are civilizations that never named their gods or attempted to portray them— at least this is what is said about the ancient Pelasgians. The Romans themselves, for at least two centuries, did not portray their deities."[3]

Parahistorians are not ordinary Japanese people. They know a lot about the stories of the enshrined kami, and in fact there is much more mythology in the parahistories than can possibly be covered in this book. The *Kujiki* and *Hotsuma Tsutaye* especially cannot be explained without mythology, so a very brief rundown of principal Japanese myths is now necessary. We begin in the "age of the kami," or *kamiyo* 神代, defined as the period before the kami descended to Earth.

A Very Fast Summary of the History of Everything

In the beginning the Earth was without form. The first thing in the world was spontaneously generated in the heavenly realm of *Takamagahara*. In the *Nihon Shoki* we are told that a World-Egg separated into *yin* and *yang* portions. The yin (female) part became heavy and naturally sank, while the yang (male) part became light and rose, generating the first kami. This is pure Taoism, so this story is assumed to have Chinese influence. In the *Kojiki,* which we assume to be older, the first thing that appears in Takamagahara is a floating mass comparable to a jellyfish. From this, the first kami sprout like reeds.[4]

The initial kami are said to have ruled the universe with three generations of male kami and four generations of joint male-female rule, but other than that there is not much that can be said about them. The first important myth is the story of Izanagi and Izanami. The two of them, male and female, descend to Earth on divine command. They walk in ritual form around a pillar reaching up to heaven and greet each other. "Oh, what a lovely man!" says Izanami. "Oh, what a lovely girl!" says Izanagi, but mutters to himself, "It is not proper that the woman spoke first." They make children, but the first time the ritual doesn't work and the child, Hiruko, is small and weak. The two of them return to Takamagahara to consult with the kami, and a divination is performed. The kami learn that the man was supposed to speak first in the ritual. They come back down and repeat the ritual properly with Izanagi confessing first, and Izanami bears a total of fourteen great islands and thirty-five kami.

Thus, the Japanese histories do not begin with the world being completely ordered, but with an unwritten rule being broken. It seems that even the ancestors in Takamagahara are unclear on these rules, and must perform divination to understand how to set things right. This was clearly an honest mistake on Izanami's part and does not amount to her being blamed or attacked. Rather, she and Izanagi seem to be a happy couple. There is even an element of humor in the whole thing since the two of them are sent down on a universe-creating mission but mess it up through all-too-human error, and the historian dutifully includes this in his narrative. Anyway, they do it properly the second time and all is forgiven as the world itself is produced: Izanami gives birth to all the islands of Japan.

The last kami born to Izanami is Fire. Fire burns her body, and she dies, causing Izanagi to weep in despair, mourn her, and bury her. His grief is unbearable and he descends into the netherworld, called *Yomi* in Japanese, to see her again. Izanagi meets Izanami's spirit and begs her to return. She is delighted to see him but tells him that she had already eaten the food of the netherworld and cannot return. She bids him to wait patiently while she consults with the lords of Yomi, but he cannot restrain himself and breaks into the inner sanctum only to see her rotting corpse covered in maggots, which produce more kami. Izanami's spirit, filled with shame, rages against Izanagi and chases him to the surface, where he fights her off by throwing peaches at her. She vows to bring death to the world as revenge.

Izanagi, after washing off the stench of Yomi in a river and thereby producing more kami, chooses his three most promising children to inherit the "heavenly realms." Amaterasu, whose name means "light of heaven" and who is usually understood to be a female representation of the sun, is given "knowledge" (usually translated as *sovereignty*) of Takamagahara.[5] Tsukuyomi, the "moon reader" of unknown sex, is given knowledge of the "realms of the night" and then vanishes from the narrative. Finally, Susanowo, a male kami with an obscure name, is given knowledge of the ocean. Susanowo, however, refuses to rule his realm with dignity and angers his father by crying and saying he wants to visit "the land of his mother," so Izanagi banishes him from the country, to which he has given the name "Shiwa-Kami-Hotsuma" (later renamed Akitsushima, Yamato, Nihon, and finally Japan).

But the petulant Susanowo refuses to leave immediately, instead declaring that he wants to say goodbye to Amaterasu. Suspecting trouble, she binds her hair and readies her bow and quivers, greeting her brother in full warrior dress. Susanowo, apparently annoyed by this, informs her that his intentions are pure* and demonstrates by producing kami from his spit, which grow into beautiful maidens. Gleeful for having proven himself, he wreaks havoc and defecates all over Amaterasu's palace and tears up her fields, but Amaterasu refuses to get angry, instead saying:

> That which appears to be faeces must be what my brother has vomited and strewn around while drunk. Also his breaking down the ridges of the paddies and covering up their ditches—my brother must have done this because he thought it was wasteful to use the land thus.[6]

---

*Literally, "my heart is red." In Old Japanese the word "red" meant bright and pure. This seems to survive today in the color used in the national flag.

This response appears to be an example of *kotodama,* the spirit created by language that Shintoists see as an extremely powerful, magical tool. Here Amaterasu's speech is described as *nori-naoshi,* correcting the situation through carefully chosen words. This healing kotodama should allow an opening for Susanowo to slow down and reflect on his deeds. Unfortunately, it just makes him angrier out of spite, and his rage increases.

The frightened Amaterasu secludes herself in a cave, plunging Japan into total darkness. Now Takamagahara is cast into pandemonium and all the kami convene to determine how to lure her out. A divination and ceremony is held by the door, and in the *Nihon Shoki* Amaterasu's heart is soothed by their kind and respectful appeals. In the *Kojiki,* however, things are trickier. A kami named Uzume strips off her clothes and begins to dance, while the other kami cheer her on and play music. Amaterasu, finding the sounds most curious, peeks out of the cave to see what all the fuss is about. The kami lure her with a mirror, then pull her out and ritually seal the cave. This legend of the rock cave is one of the most heavily analyzed Japanese myths and has been a focus for interpreters since at least the tenth century.

Susanowo is tarred and feathered and cast out to the Izumo region of Japan, but at this point we must leave the age of the kami behind. The Izumo cycle is equally fascinating (Susanowo notably slays an eight-headed snake) but does not enter into any of the parahistories in this book. Today, the Izumo area of Japan remains influenced by Susanowo and is considered to have a very dangerous power: visiting the Izumo Grand Shrine by yourself is very effective to help you find a life partner, but visiting it with an unmarried partner will create bad energy between you.

W. G. Aston's *Nihongi* (1896) is the authoritative translation of the *Nihon Shoki* and is available for free online for those who want to pursue these legends further. Unfortunately I cannot offer such a source for the *Kojiki.* Basil Hall Chamberlain's translation should be avoided, and Donald L. Philippi's excellent translation has been out of print for half a century and is now quite rare.

The First Emperors

Amaterasu's grandson, Ninigi, receives an edict to take on human form and descend from Takamagahara to a place called Takachiho on the island of Kyushu. Ninigi takes a wife and populates the island. In 660 BCE (1,792,470 years later) his descendant hears a rumor that "the center of the world" is located somewhere far to the east and conquers this wonderful land, becoming the first Emperor, Jimmu. Note that according to the *Nihon Shoki* Emperor Jimmu is not the only descendant from Takamagahara in the seventh century BCE. The people he conquers, the Mononobe clan, are acknowledged to be descended from someone named Nigihayahi who came down from Takamagahara in a flying ship (see chapters 2 and 4). Indeed, the Emperor himself says, "There are many other children of the Heavenly Kami," and willingly accepts a rival claim to divine descent.[7]

Emperor Jimmu possibly has equal rank with other descendants, but he has divine right to rule Japan, as demonstrated by several signs. A strange sword, which is itself called a kami, is given to him by a man from Kumano who says he found it on his roof—recalling the ancient belief, which was once prevalent throughout the world, in "thunder stones" thrown down by the gods with lightning bolts. Indeed, the Emperor speaks of a dream in which the kami sent him this sword. A three-legged crow called Yatagarasu, a fisherman who is called a kami, and a man with a tail who lives in a well all appear, declaring they will help him. In classical Japan influential families claimed to descend from all of these beings, including the crow.[8]

Emperor Jimmu subdues his enemies with grace, builds a palace, and settles down with a lovely empress in the Yamato region. In the *Nihon Shoki* he makes remarkably Chinese-style remarks about the importance of peaceful government, filial piety, and respecting the ancestors. In the *Kojiki* there is no such Chinese influence. Instead Jimmu is reported to have composed some short songs for his wife, such as the following:

> *In a humble little house,*
> *Nestling in a reed-plain,*

Spreading out the clean
Rustling sedge-mats,
The two of us slept.[9]

Over time the record of emperors after Jimmu becomes steadily less full of revelations and strange happenings. In the *Nihon Shoki* Emperor Suinin (29 BCE–70 CE) is instructed by Amaterasu to build a shrine to her "in the province of Ise, of the divine wind," which she also calls "the land whither repair the waves from Tokoyo." The shrine the Emperor builds is currently the most important shrine in the country. Called Ise Jingū, it consists of the outer palace or Gekū, built for the kami Toyouke, and the inner palace or Naikū, built for Amaterasu herself. The Tokoyo, "distant land" or "eternal world," that they face was apparently located over the ocean somewhere to the east of Japan. Commentators believe Tokoyo to be a "fairyland."[10]

Emperor Keiko (71–130 CE) will provide us with one final aside, not for anything special he did but because of his son Prince Wousu. One day the Emperor asks his son to admonish his elder brother for not showing up for dinner. Wousu does so by breaking his brother's bones and pulling off his limbs. The terrified Emperor tells his son to go subdue some insolent clans in the west, apparently out of the belief that Wousu would not come back alive. Instead, the prince deceives and kills a number of different enemies, outwits a traitorous lord, and has six children by six different women. For this he is given the well-deserved name Yamato-Takeru, meaning Hero (or Brave Man) of the Yamato. There is no one else like Yamato-Takeru in the official histories, although many families claimed descent from him.

And there you have it: the official histories through the second century CE. To be fair, the same documents continue into the seventh century and become much more useful for historians and textbooks later on. Some of the final chapters are still taught in schools, since they contain, for example, our only records of Prince Shōtoku. But these initial stories lack internal consistency and many specifics. How, for example, are kami created from other kami? Why did Amaterasu own paddies and fields for Susanowo to trample on? Was there rice farming or an imperial palace in her era? Why did the kami "descend" to Earth when they already appeared to be there, and what were the other divine descendants doing in the age of Emperor Jimmu? Can we honestly call this a record or chronicle of things that really happened, and if not, how should we view these stories? Why were two large variants written in such a short space of time? The classical Japanese may have possessed some knowledge of these matters; for the average modern reader these questions cannot be answered.

FUTOMANI, THE SCRIPT OF THE GODS, AND KOTODAMA

From the 1600s on some Japanese people have been engaged in a quest to understand their origins, trying to uncover the *true* Japan prior to its language and mythology intermingling with Chinese sources. Parahistory is part of this quest. This does not mean that parahistories are antagonistic toward other countries, but the Japan they envision is a country of its own, so many of them employ the concept of *Ko-Shinto,* the imagined "ways of the kami" from before they were submerged in Taoist and Buddhist language.

Ko-Shinto is quite a difficult topic to untangle. If any of the parahistories are true, they can give us accurate information about Ko-Shinto, but without that assumption there are no written sources for us to rely on and most people are simply offering their personal opinions. We can be reasonably certain that the ancient Japanese envisioned a ball-shaped soul called *tamashii* and a heavenly, distant realm above the Earth because the descriptions of these in the *Kojiki* do not resemble Chinese mythology. Other than that, the only definite aspect of Ko-Shinto that is affirmed by archaeology is *futomani*.

Futomani is a mysterious method of divination found at the very beginning of the *Kojiki* and *Nihon Shoki*. When Izanami and Izanagi fail to create a child, they ascend from the earthly realm to the heavenly realm, and the heavenly kami perform futomani to understand what went wrong. When Amaterasu hides in the rock cave, the kami Futotama performs a divination, which the *Nihon Shoki* calls *futomani,* and which the *Kojiki* says involved roasting the shoulder bone of a stag and observing the cracks that form. Archaeological evidence shows that the ancient Japanese really did perform such stag divination hundreds of years before foreign immigration.[11]

Futomani is generally identified with this Jōmon period stag divination, but if you read the above account very closely, you will see that this connection is not explicit. As we will see nearly all the parahistories incorporate futomani in some way. Some explain how readings should be interpreted, but none of them explicitly say what sort of object is read to do the divination. Oddly, there has been very little written about futomani by anyone whatsoever outside of parahistories. Even if we question the provenance of these documents they remain important primary sources for futomani.

Kamiyo Moji

Kamiyo moji, or *jindai moji,* are literally the "scripts of the age of the kami." This refers to a belief, attested since medieval times, that the ancient kami of Japan had their own indigenous system of writing that they must have needed to perform futomani. Academics identify futomani with stag divination, which is not known to have used a writing system, but as we have seen above these links are tenuous.

The existence of kamiyo moji was first established in a major thirteenth-century commentary on the *Nihon Shoki* called *Shaku Nihongi.* After commenting on the futomani story, it claims that kamiyo moji from Hi province, now Nagasaki and Saga prefectures, could still be found in the imperial library. From the very beginning, then, kamiyo moji are not just a hypothetical suggestion, but are claimed to still be present in Japan. A later commentary on the *Nihon Shoki*, written in 1527 by Nobukata Kiyohara, states: "The script of the kami age has been hidden away. There are 15,379 undisseminated characters." The author of this book was a respected scholar writing a historical treatise and had no apparent reason to randomly interject a false statistic in the middle of his book.

Why did kamiyo moji disappear? The famous early modern philologist Atsutane Hirata, looking into this very question, heard a legend from the Urabe family, an old household of soothsayers. According to them kamiyo moji was known to at least a few literate elders up until the early 500s. At that point Buddhism was introduced to Japan, and powerful clans adopted the Buddha as a foreign spiritual force more powerful than the native kami. The first Buddhist emperor, Kinmei, who reigned from 539–571 CE banned the kamiyo moji and ordered his courtier Tokiwa no Ōmuraji to rewrite Japan's ancient literature in Chinese characters. For this reason, an Inbe clan elder writing a history called *Kogo Shūi* purposefully claimed in 808 that "in days of yore, there was no script; words and deeds of men were remembered solely by mouth." If there was anyone who knew of the existence of an old script, they were definitely not allowed to write about it.

From that era until the Edo period, to be educated in Japan meant being Buddhist, and it is easy to understand that this group would laugh off any claims that Japan had its own writing system before the arrival of Buddhism. The people of Japan came to believe that their entire literary culture was derived from China, a country that even today calls itself the "Middle Country" at the center of the Earth. It took the arrival of Western merchants, missionaries, and colonists to clear up the misconception that China was at the center of everything. With that radical change came a renewed interest in understanding Japan's uniqueness.

Texts bearing kamiyo moji have been found in the treasure houses of scattered shrines throughout Japan. There were already dozens of them in existence in the eighteenth century, a startling fact by itself. If the kamiyo moji have no basis in history, why were so many independent people driven to invent them? Late in that century Atsutane Hirata closely investigated the subject and concluded that most of the scripts were forgeries. The script that he found the most frequently he dubbed Ahiru script (fig. 1.3), and he decided that it was probably the most authentic option. However, modern researchers cannot take this script seriously, because it looks similar to the Korean *Hangul* script, and its orthography is the same as modern Japanese even though ancient Japanese is thought to have been quite different. Research has shown that Ahiru script is not attested before medieval times. Hirata can be forgiven this error, because he was one of the first philologists in Japan, but modern scholars disagree with his verdict. Again, the appearance of Ahiru script across the country in the medieval era, without any original text to attest for it before Hirata's study, is an odd phenomenon indeed. The persistent legend of the kamiyo moji, which even today has its proponents, will lead us directly into the world of parahistory.

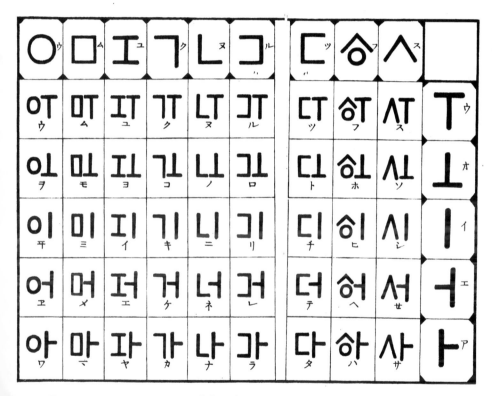

Figure 1.3. Atsutane Hirata believed this Ahiru script was used in the Age of the Gods. From Kanna Hifumi no Tsutae *(1819).*

김지환은 역사상 최강의 전사

Figure 1.4. Example of Korean Hangul script.

FURTHER READING
ON JAPANESE HISTORY

The following English sources are recommended for further investigation of kami and early records:

Nihongi, translated by W. G. Aston (Japan Society, 1896). Available online at www.archive.org.

Kojiki, translated by Donald L. Philippi (University of Tokyo Press, 1968, out of print).

A New History of Shinto, by John Breen and Mark Teeuwen (Wiley-Blackwell, 2010).

Before the Nation: Kokugaku and the Imagining of Community in Early Modern Japan, by Susan L. Burns (Duke University Press, 2003).

Himiko and Japan's Elusive Chiefdom of Yamatai, by J. Edward Kidder (University of Hawaii Press, 2007).

A Year in the Life of a Shinto Shrine, by John K. Nelson (University of Washington Press, 1996).

Japan in Five Ancient Chinese Chronicles: Wo, the Land of Yamatai, and Queen Himiko, translated by Massimo Soumare and Davide Mana (Kurodahan Press, 2009).

Tsubaki Grand Shrine of America (www.tsubakishrine.org) has an active Facebook group.

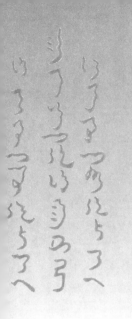

2
Prince Shōtoku's
Lost Classic

Sendai Kuji Hongi Taiseikyō

So far, we have been traveling through an altogether comfortable area of Japanese mythology and philology. Now we begin to set out on the adventure of parahistory. But one does not simply step over a line from a well-known course into unexplored territory. We must first leave the beaten track and head down a little-known side trail, familiar to a small number of classicists but rarely traveled to its end. We might be able to fill some of the huge gaps left by the *Kojiki* and *Nihon Shoki* and glean some lost information about ancient Japan if we possessed some of the records of the Mononobe clan, that rival tribe whose patriarch descended from heaven in a flying ship. In fact a little-known ancient text with strong links to the Mononobe does exist: the *Sendai Kuji Hongi,* also called *Kujiki.* It is in the uncertainty and intrigue surrounding this book that the first parahistory emerges.

The title *Sendai Kuji Hongi* appears in the *Nihon Shoki*'s biography of Prince Shōtoku, a hero of the early classical age. The Prince was the author of a ranking system for the imperial court and commentaries on Buddhist philosophy. He famously ranked the Emperor of China by sending a convoy bearing "greetings from the Emperor of the land where the sun rises, to the Emperor of the land where the sun sets," and in doing so coined Japan's modern name, Nihon, the Land of the Rising Sun. He also wrote an eloquent and forthright edict entitled the Seventeen-Article Constitution, which encourages court officials to revere the Buddha, seek harmony, reward goodness, and avoid attention seeking. Legend has it that he was able to hear seven different people talking to him at once and resolve all of their problems with warmth and justice. Like King Solomon, he was a wise lord with a touch of genius.

Prince Shōtoku lived in an era of upheaval when the warlike rhetoric of rivaling doctrines and tribes, some of native stock and some from overseas, threatened to tear apart the nation. Somehow he fashioned a rule for the entire nation of Japan that all the different tribes and doctrines could unite under. It would seem to make sense that he would want to resolve the conflicts between tribal legends with one authoritative, national history as well. Indeed, it is written in the *Nihon Shoki* that Prince Shōtoku had authored a history of Japan in 620 CE, but this document was burned in 645 during a coup. Its replacement, of course, is the *Nihon Shoki* itself, which makes the story slightly suspicious.

A tantalizing possibility presents itself: What if someone had saved a copy of Prince Shōtoku's history somewhere? Would the great prince be able to resolve the contradictions between the *Kojiki* and the *Nihon Shoki* and shed light on the puzzles of ancient Japanese legends? In fact, there are several documents claiming to be this lost history, and some of them have such broad scholarly support that they are arguably not even parahistory. So, depending on who you ask, the first parahistory can be traced to 620 CE, 710, 936, 1670, 1679, or later, and it might consist of ten, thirty, thirty-one, thirty-eight, or seventy-two volumes. But the seventy-two-volume version we will explore in this chapter is unique—it claims to be not merely the work of Shōtoku, but a compilation of texts from the Age of the Gods. What's more, it has a deep connection to a modern revelation called *Hitsuki Shinji*.

LOST TO HISTORY,
FOUND BY TROUBLEMAKERS

In 936 a scholar named Yatabe no Kinmochi claimed at a customary conference on the *Nihon Shoki* that he had in his possession a copy of Prince Shōtoku's lost history, which he then quoted from. Yatabe claimed further that this document, the *Sendai Kuji Hongi,* was actually the basis for the *Kojiki* and *Nihon Shoki.* If this document were real, the entire history of Japan could be turned upside down. Little more was heard about it, though, until the Middle Ages.

Professor Hideki Saitō of Bukkyō University considers the *Kujiki* a herald of the end of the classical era. The fact that the organizers of a tenth-century conference devoted to the *Nihon Shoki* could allow someone to wave around a copy of a completely different history text and claim it was older and more accurate than the *Nihon Shoki* can mean only one thing: the *Nihon Shoki* itself was not answering all the questions of a Japanese society that was rapidly changing and was even moving away from the production of official imperial chronicles.[1]

What secrets could Prince Shōtoku's *Sendai Kuji Hongi* conceal? Confounding the scholars, there are no fewer than five different documents that claim to be the ancient text Yatabe no Kinmochi had cited. Following parahistorical practice I will refer to the different documents based on the number of volumes their original manuscripts contained:

Kujiki-10 (that is, the *Kujiki* in ten volumes): widely quoted since 936, exists in medieval manuscripts.
Kujiki-31: first appeared in 1670, is also called the Sasakiden.
Kujiki-38: allegedly existed before 1679, is also called the Kōyabon.
Kujiki-72: first appeared in 1679, is also called the Enpōhan or Chouonbon.
Kujiki-30: first appeared in the 1720s, is also called the Shirakawaden or Hakkebon.

Note that all of these documents claim to have been written in 620 CE.

I will deal with the *Kujiki*-10 first, since its text was known centuries before the other versions. It is mostly similar to the *Kojiki* and *Nihon Shoki,* with only a few notable exceptions, one being that unlike the two official histories with their spontaneous generation of a heavenly realm, the *Kujiki*-10 opens with a single Creator Kami making the universe. The Creator Kami appears alone before generating a male and female pair to lead the second generation. Another difference is that the *Kujiki*-10 tells the story of Nigihayahi (the rival claimant to divine descent) in greater detail. We learn that Nigihayahi, like Emperor Jimmu, had a special grant from the kami and was given a set of mysterious treasures, which will be discussed later. But other than that the main lesson the *Kujiki*-10 has for us is that modern scholars have incorrectly labeled it a forgery, which is something to keep in mind when looking at later parahistories.

Since the eighteenth century Japanese philologists have frequently attacked the *Kujiki*-10 for reasons that will become clear below, but the few reputable Western scholars of the Japanese classics believe that the *Kujiki*-10 really is a forgotten history of Japan and predates both the *Nihon Shoki* and *Kojiki*. The most notable of these are W. G. Aston, who relied on it heavily for his 1896 translation of the *Nihon Shoki* and commented that the *Kujiki*-10 "ought to be translated," G. Walter Robinson who demonstrated evidence of its authenticity in 1955, and John R. Bentley of Northern Illinois University who in 2006 finally produced a full analysis and translation.[2]

Professor Bentley's work shows that the *Kujiki*-10 passes sophisticated linguistic tests and does appear to be a precursor to the *Nihon Shoki,* having been written around 680–710. But, because it was never completed and has been tampered with by many hands, it was incorrectly ascribed to Prince Shōtoku centuries later. Even as scholars admit most of Professor Bentley's facts, though, an official redating of the *Kujiki*-10 seems beyond the pale. It would require completely rethinking how these three histories were compiled and would give more weight to the *Nihon Shoki* and less to the *Kojiki*, revealing the instability of academic proposals about Japanese ancient history. The *Kojiki* actually has many of the same authenticity issues as the *Kujiki*-10 and some scholars still claim it is a forgery.[3]

Both Professor Bentley and other Western and Eastern scholars over the past century have resolved the anachronisms of the *Kujiki*-10 by positing an "Ur-*Kujiki*" from which the *Kujiki*-10 was redacted. At least three unredacted texts appeared in the seventeenth and eighteenth centuries, all of which claim the title of *Taiseikyō,* or *Complete Version,* the original text from before later scribes edited it down. In other words, they claim to be the document that scholars are looking for! But the way in which these texts appeared is not straightforward at all. In fact, we might recognize this story as symptomatic of the genre that it birthed.

An Auspicious Meeting

The year was 1667 and the influential Kyoto intellectual and Zen monk Dōkai Chouon had just authored a commentary on Prince Shōtoku's Seventeen-Article Constitution as described in the *Nihon Shoki*. One day his monastery was paid a visit by a strange little man calling himself Ikeda the Recluse, about whom we know virtually nothing.

"I read erewhile your Treatise on Prince Shōtoku's Constitution," said the recluse. "But know ye of Prince Shōtoku's Constitution for the Monks?"

"I know not," said the monk, "nor have I heard of it."

"Even if you should see it," Ikeda remarked, "you will surely call it *Forgery.*" And with that, he left. Chouon's interest was somehow piqued.

Next, Chouon spoke with Kuranosuke Kyōgoku, a local publisher who had recently privately printed an expanded version of the *Kujiki* in thirty-one volumes. For unknown reasons Kyōgoku made woodblocks of this book at very great expense, but printed so few copies of it that only a single copy in the treasure house of Ise Jingū is known to historians today. This *Kujiki*-31 at Ise Jingū is not particularly controversial in its contents, but apparently it has ten additional books that are not available to the public (which would make it the *Kujiki-41* if they are ever released). It is not clear why Ise Jingū continues to conceal ten books of a medieval history text in the present day.[4]

Chouon asked about Ikeda's odd reference and Kyōgoku informed him that Prince Shōtoku had written not one but five constitutions, two of which were the *Nihon Shoki* version and the Buddhist ordinances Ikeda had mentioned. He then explained that these were contained in the complete version of Shōtoku's *Kujiki* that had recently been rediscovered in a shrine called Izawa-no-miya by someone named Uneme Nagano. He showed Chouon a copy of his *Kujiki,* but told him that he would have to read Nagano's complete copy and talk with him to understand its full import.

This Nagano was regarded as an eccentric polymath and teacher of sorts, and either his parents named him Uneme, "servant-woman of the Emperor," or he changed his own name to this for unexplained, esoteric reasons. When Chouon met Nagano not only did he learn of Prince Shōtoku's long-suppressed knowledge, but the monk was so impressed by the teacher's intellect that he actually became Nagano's disciple and received esoteric initiation from him.[5]

With Chouon's help Shōtoku's true Five Constitutions were published in Edo (i.e., Tokyo) in 1675 and were widely appreciated. In that era Buddhists, Shintoists, and Confucianists were accusing each other of ignorance and denying each other's teachings, but in the Five Constitutions Prince Shōtoku informed them that each teaching had its place in life and Japan needed all three teachings, like a chair needs three legs to stand. It seemed as if Shōtoku had specifically written these Constitutions to resolve Japan's weightiest intellectual conflicts with the goal of encouraging unselfish operation of the state.

Obviously the time was ripe to release Shōtoku's long-forgotten true history, and in 1679 Chouon was able to publish the full seventy-two-volume edition of the *Kujiki* that Nagano had found at Izawa-no-miya (fig. 2.1). Teachers, monks, scholars, and intellectuals of all stripes were delighted by the new ancient text. Japan's bookish philologists were constantly bickering about which variation of the *Nihon Shoki* was cor-

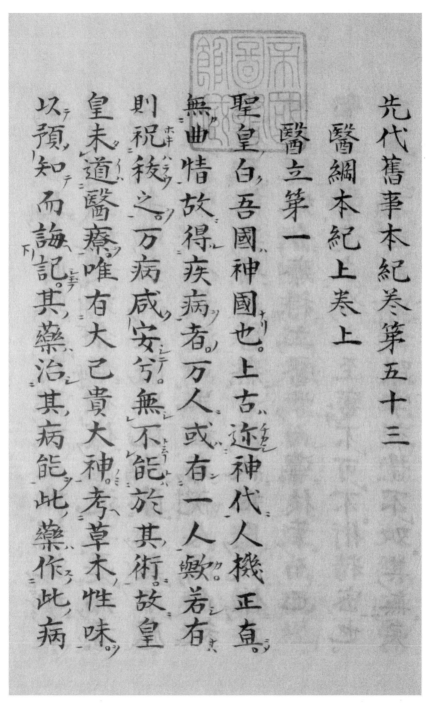

先代舊事本紀卷第五十三

醫綱本紀上卷上

醫立第一

聖皇白吾國神國也。上古迩神代人機正直。
無曲情故得疾病者。万人或有一人歟若有
則祝祓之。万病咸安兮。無不能於其術。故皇
皇未道醫療。唯有大己貴大神。考草木性味。
以預知而誨記。其藥治其病能此。藥作此病

Figure 2.1. The opening pages of book 53 of the Kujiki-72 *describing laws of medicine. (Courtesy National Diet Library.)*

rect, but the *Kujiki*-72 claimed to be an older and more accurate history, written by the great Prince Shōtoku no less.

Then, right at the height of the text's popularity, tragedy struck: to Chouon's shock government authorities banned the documents and charged *him* with conspiracy and forgery. To understand why this happened we have to backtrack a little and learn more about this Izawa-no-miya.

The Shrine Workers' Revenge

Japan's Warring States period was a time of unprecedented devastation around the country. No one was safe from the violence, not even the sacred sites. Temples trained their monks to be warriors, and shrines were burned to the ground. Even Ise Jingū, the ancient shrine of the imperial family and arguably the single most sacred place in Japan, had to suspend its ageless rites for the first time ever and lost the strength to support and defend its three auxiliary shrines located to its south and west. One of the auxiliary shrines, Izawa-no-miya (fig. 2.2), fell to the Kuki clan in 1531. The Kuki killed Izawa's head ritualist and ransacked the shrine, seizing the surrounding villages for themselves. The shrine employees, called *jinnin*, hid the ancient manuscripts and treasures of Izawa-no-miya in their households and waited for the day when things would be set right.

In the 1600s the Tokugawa shogunate rose to power and put an end to the constant fighting, but the Izawa-no-miya area remained under Kuki control, and the vassals became disgruntled. The disaffected jinnin petitioned the shogun repeatedly to return the sacred land and allow the shrine to be rebuilt and maintained. The appeals began in 1632 and escalated year by year afterward, with some jinnin traveling as far as Edo. Meanwhile, the Kuki samurai simply ignored Izawa-no-miya and let it fall into disrepair.

The vassals, being employees of Japan's most important shrine complex, had a strong sense of justice, but both secular and spiritual authorities were uncomfortable. The fields around Izawa produced some of the most bountiful rice harvests anywhere in Japan. Indeed, crops from

Figure 2.2. Izawa-no-miya, where the first parahistory was revealed.

these fields had always been donated to Ise Jingū, and the *Nihon Shoki* says that Yamatohime-no-mikoto, daughter of the legendary Emperor Suinin (29 BCE–70 CE) and sometimes identified with Himiko of the Yamatai narrative, founded Izawa-no-miya herself to provide nourishment for Amaterasu. On one hand, the shrine was clearly sacred and needed to be treated properly. But on the other hand, recognizing that the shrine was important enough to be restored to its retainers would have meant seizing a wealthy area from a powerful clan. Even Ise Jingū sided with the Kuki claim simply to stay on the shogun's side in a still delicate situation. So, local authorities stonewalled, and the appeals continued fruitlessly for over a decade.

In the late 1640s a twist was added to the story: the shrine workers began to claim that Izawa-no-miya was not just an auxiliary shrine but in fact was the oldest part of Ise Jingū and was of prime spiritual importance. In one petition to Jingū authorities, dated August 1648, they wrote, "Izawa-no-Miya is called one of the 'Three Shrines of Ise' with the Naikū and Gekū, a 'Place of the Way' hidden in the innermost reaches of the Naikū." The terms *Three Shrines of Ise* and *Place of the Way* had never been seen before by anyone, but the jinnin had written proof in documents they had found among the shrine's treasures. For over a decade more and more documents attesting to the ancient doctrine of the Three Shrines of Ise were produced and sent to the shogun, the Emperor, the Jingū, and everyone else, and finally in 1661, after countless rejected appeals and ignored petitions, Izawa-no-miya was restored to its rightful owners.[6]

Now, here's the rub: The jinnin were still making a fuss about the documents they had found, and the *Kujiki-72*, which was found at Izawa-no-miya, claims that Izawa-no-miya is the oldest part of Ise Jingū. The Three Shrines of Ise doctrine was thus propagated throughout literary circles in the country. Following complaints from Ise Jingū authorities, the hammer came down, and fast. In June 1681, just two years after its publication, the shogunate announced that the *Kujiki-72* and the other documents were forgeries written by Nagano and Chouon with input from the Izawa-no-miya shrine workers, and ordered them both imprisoned.

The Shogun Runs Scared

Chouon and Nagano refused to stand down. Instead, they published a pamphlet asserting that no matter what anyone said the *Kujiki-72* was a real ancient document, and that they had no connections to Izawa-no-miya (which seems to be true*). Once again the shogun reacted severely. Nagano and his family were exiled to a distant part of Japan and died there. Chouon escaped such severe punishment thanks to his connections in the aristocracy, but never spoke of the *Kujiki-72* again. Nearly all copies of the *Kujiki-72* and the blocks used to print it were destroyed, and the

---

*Uneme Nagano stood accused of being an employee of Izawa-no-miya, but there is no evidence of this; on the contrary, his biographer tells us that he was actually living in a completely different region before he came to Kyoto. The same document tells us that Nagano's family possessed some ancient Mononobe texts; the relation of these to the *Kujiki-72* is unclear. (From Senrei, *Nagano Uneme Den*.)

text was only reconstructed from partial copies in the twentieth century.[7]

Rather than ending the matter by punishing the supposed forgers, though, the shogunate put a ban on all usage of the *Kujiki*—nobody was allowed to quote the forbidden text at all. Clearly this was not a simple case of falsehood exposed, as it was with great Western forgeries like the Roman Catholics' Donation of Constantine. Even after the government experts laid down their official ruling, they remained somehow frightened by what might come from continued discussion of the matter. The censorship remained in place for more than 150 years, possibly up until the end of the Tokugawa regime.

Meanwhile, the *Kujiki*-72 had opened the door to what became a new paradigm of analysis. In 1736 Yukikazu Yoshimi deduced that one of the two main shrines at Ise Jingū, the Gekū, had been perpetuating several forgeries to trump up the importance of its kami, and the nature of Japan's greatest shrine was forever transformed. Soon afterward, the original *Kujiki*-10 was claimed by a member of the Tokugawa clan to have also been forged to empower the Gekū. This sloppy theory was clearly a result of zealotry following the *Kujiki*-72 incident. While the anachronistic preface to the *Kujiki*-10 was apparently written by someone related to the Gekū, its contents were not. But this, too, became a standard revision of the traditional understanding.[8]

In 1763 Norinaga Motoori announced that he, like Chouon before him, had found an older text than the *Nihon Shoki* with its many variants. Motoori's text, the *Kojiki*, withstood the shogun's scrutiny, but that regime could not have predicted what would happen next. In a monumental achievement, remembered as one of the greatest moments in Japanese history, Motoori united philologists under his Kokugaku school and turned the study of that single history into a rebirth of Japan's self-image that rallied the people around the Emperor and eventually created modern Japan.

Decades after the controversy died down an odd footnote arose in this story. Although public discussion of the *Kujiki* was banned, in the eighteenth century the Shirakawa clan began privately circulating the ancient documents of their own household, which I have dubbed the *Kujiki*-30. They claimed *this* was the true writing of Prince Shōtoku and that Nagano had shamefully tampered with it to insert his eclectic prophecies and philosophies. But because of official censorship their text was never printed. A small group of supporters today have partial manuscripts to work with.

The Forgery Theory Collapses

It is admittedly all too easy for establishment historians to stand by the government verdict of forgery, but it is also overly simplistic because, as explained above, the *Kujiki*-72 is only one of several *Kujiki* texts that came to light in the seventeenth century. Besides the *Kujiki*-31, a monk at Mount Kōya owned a different history-only *Kujiki* with thirty-eight volumes, which is no longer extant, but which professor Seizō Kōno believed was used as the historical section of the *Kujiki*-72. This seems to open the gate to speculation: If there were at least two extra *Kujiki*s floating around in the 1670s, who is to say there were not more? Remember that the *Kujiki*-10 is generally acknowledged to contain useful information despite the verdict of "forgery," and it is thought to have relied on real ancient sources. Could the *Kujiki*-72 have been compiled in a similar way?

That Chouon and Nagano's publication was of a completely different nature from the others is clear. The text is of dubious historical accuracy, but its accuracy on other matters makes it easy to understand why it was valued so highly by scholars and considered so dangerous by the authorities. As a twentieth century researcher said "I want to make clear now, to prevent misunderstanding, that I am not evaluating this book's historical value or anything like that. What I am trying to say in this book is that it has far greater value than that."[9]

THE SECRET TEACHINGS
OF THE ANCIENT EMPERORS

In the preface to the *Kujiki*-72 Prince Shōtoku explains he had concerns, like ours, about the lack of documentation from the Age of the Kami and requested the various clans reveal whatever secret texts they had. Members of the Inbe and Urabe diviner clans responded to his plea. It turns out they knew of a set of "clay urns" (recalling the clay work of the Jōmon period), which possessed documents from the age of Emperor Jimmu, some of which were bestowed on Jimmu by the kami and written in Japan's native script—the kamiyo moji. Following the clans' instructions, courtiers made a visit to an obscure place called the Shrine of A-Wa and found the clay urns buried in the ground there.

Through careful study of these secret texts and others available in the imperial household, Prince Shōtoku came to understand the underlying messages and principles beneath the Japanese mythological world, enabling him to explain how these early events were not just a matter of storytelling or cause and effect but demonstrated the ability of the human actors to discern perennial truths. The preface states: "In this world, ways are constructed from the choices of men. If we cannot discuss these actions we will not know the Way." For example, Amaterasu's hiding in the rock cave and plunging the Earth into darkness established the rule that a king who lacks "heavenly wisdom" will surely plunge his kingdom into darkness, and when Amano-omoikane summoned the Long-Crying Bird to bring Amaterasu back to the surface, the rule was established that he who possesses natural law will conquer.[10]

Prince Shōtoku learned the meaning of right government from these texts, developing five Seventeen-Article Constitutions from their principles, and he rendered them into Classical Chinese for future generations. But Shōtoku lived in a degenerate age when history was being distorted, and he foresaw that he would not be able to publish what he had learned without repercussions. The preface laments that "historians in this age have added their biases and concealed, but nobody yet has recorded the facts as they are without taking sides. With time, the truth that we know will be lost, and posterity will be built on a foundation of our lies." Therefore, when the *Kujiki*-72 was completed it was hidden in three locations: Ise Jingū, Ōmiwa

Jinja, and Shitennō Temple. Presumably Izawa-no-miya was part of Ise Jingū at the time.

The *Kujiki*-72 takes us from the Age of the Kami, through the Age of the Emperors, to the present day in 620. At the end of the history, from books 35 to 38, we are offered a supernatural hagiography of Prince Shōtoku himself, making the claim that the Prince edited the books a little strange. The second half of the *Kujiki*-72, though, is most interesting—it is a compilation of all the ancient wisdom available in 620, accompanied by teachings based on these principles. For example, books 47 and 48 lay out the process of futomani divination, books 61 and 62 contain ancient Japanese songs, and book 69 is a book of prophecy, which some claim predicts recent history and World War III.* Books 53 to 56 describe a summary of findings about ancient medicine. We learn that sickness is caused by a climate of dishonesty and untruth, that the people in the Age of the Kami avoided illness entirely through honest and frank attitudes, and that if anyone ever got sick their hearts were purified through healing kotodama and other methods, and they would quickly recover.[11]

Recipe for a Universe

The *Kujiki*-72, like all versions of the *Kujiki,* begins with a single Creator Kami making the universe. In this version the universe itself is a manifestation of the "Uncreated Original Lord of Heaven," of whom the text says "The Creator rules over boundless infinity. Nothing existed before the Creator. No one ruled before the Creator. The Creator is without Form." This Creator manifests all the forms of the world, but we are not just talking about the material universe. Here, material conditions are much less important than the creation of immaterial things such as thoughts, languages, and the distinctions between different ideas. The components of the immaterial world are described as the Five Weights, which are:

---

*What it actually purports to be is ten centuries of prophecy covering the years 622–1622. Since the book appeared in 1672, one cannot help but feel slightly underwhelmed.

神—*Kami*

心—*Kokoro,* or Mind-Heart, the two being linked in Japanese

理—Principle, or Nature (in the sense of "behavior")

氣—*Qi,* the vital energy of all living things

境—Boundary or State, the distinctions of the sensory world

In the *Kujiki-72* the creation of the world involves these intertwined yet stable elements. In the realm of time and space kami manifests itself through our hearts and minds, making all humans linked to kami through their hearts. The heart produces our principles or natures, and our variegated natures produce the desire for action—*qi.* The movements of qi produce sensory experiences and boundaries between them, so that there is no confusion between goodness and suffering, nor life and death. Finally, and most mysteriously, when these boundaries are crossed with right mindfulness we manifest kami again—what the Buddhists call *enlightenment.* The text explains that these are all good things: kami lives, the mind rules, principles preserve, qi determines our fates, and borders create form. These subtle relations between the Five Weights are the elements of all our lives. But what does this mean in practice?

A few people wrote secret commentaries on the *Kujiki-72* after it was banned. One of them was named Sadashizu Yoda. Yoda's secret manuscripts contain ample illustrations full of alchemical symbols and a proof of the Pythagorean theorem, but their descriptions of the Five Weights are inscrutable. After several hours puzzling out the words "in *kokoro* the spirit becometh flesh, having as aspects light and void," I realized that I was not going to grasp the true depths of this text, so I will simply leave you with Yoda's depiction of the "universal kokoro" for you to figure out yourself (fig. 2.3).[12] Twentieth- and twenty-first-century books written on this subject have gotten no farther than me. Nevertheless, these Five Weights have appeared in another modern document, described below.

For those like me who cannot grasp the subtle depths of the Five Weights, Prince Shōtoku points to three traditions, still extant in Japan

Figure 2.3. The universal kokoro, *according to Yoda.*

today, that can guide our day-to-day lives, not separately but together. Shinto teaches us how to relate to our past, going back to the beginning of time. Confucianism teaches us how to maintain happy and fruitful relationships in the present. Buddhism teaches us how to keep a positive attitude for the future, extending indefinitely into the afterlife. There are no conflicts between these teachings because they each have their own role in Japanese society—like a tree with Shinto being the roots, Confucianism the branches, and Buddhism the fruit. At this point in medieval Japan we find a triad of complex, possibly contradictory doctrines embraced and honored for their respective insights and spoken of as if they are interlocking parts of a higher truth—the creation of a newly balanced orthodoxy.*

---

*Even though all three of these teachings have lost their official influence in Japan, people still look to them to answer their respective uncertainties in matters of past, present, and future.

Each of these teachings has three parts—the Buddha, Dharma, and Sangha in Buddhism and the Three Bonds of ruler and subject, parent and child, and husband and wife in Confucianism. Although Shinto is not known to have three clearly identified parts, the *Kujiki-72* says that there are indeed three parts to it as well, which battled with each other in preclassical times, suddenly launching into a topic previously known only from secret doctrines.

The doctrine of three parts of Shinto is attested in the fifteenth century *Essentials of Unitary Shinto,* a frequently obscure description of an esoteric path of indeterminate age that proclaims itself a manual for one of three ways of the kami, dubbed Ancestor-Source Shinto or Sōgen 宗源. Quoting an unidentified secret text, the *Essentials* defines *Ancestor* as the "return of all phenomena to the One," and *Source* as "the unfolding of all bonds between living beings." The other two paths are called Dependent-Arising Shinto and Unified Shinto, but these are not discussed in detail. There is clearly more to this three-way division, but the deeper meanings of this manual are no longer clear to modern commentators, even those well versed in medieval Japan.[13]

In the *Kujiki-72* the terms are defined much more strictly and seem to correspond to the Taoist triad of Heaven, Earth, and Man. Here Sōgen is the path of the Seven Heavenly Deities pursued by the Urabe clan; this is surely the same Sōgen explained above. The Inbe clan, enemies of the Urabe, found their own path in Pure-Origin Shinto, or *Saigen* 斎元, which worships the Five Earthly Deities. (We may identify this with Dependent-Arising.) A third Shinto called Spirit-Ancestor, or *Reisō* 霊宗, following the Rule of the Imperial Ancestors, is proposed by Shōtoku himself as a balance: Man, between the initial two clans, Heaven and Earth. This is surely the "unified" path, and a righteous, selfless path for the Japanese nation.

The modern interpreter Takashi Gotō makes these out to be three different methods of directing one's reverence toward the past. One may turn away from the world and worship heavenly things, as in Sōgen. Or we might encourage reverence toward the visible universe and respect the Earth, as in Saigen. But in Reisō we find the world where the invisible and visible exist in harmony—that is, the world of humanity, where mind and matter interact.

Prince Shōtoku's Eighty-five-Step Path to a Better Nation

Shortly before the *Kujiki*-72 itself was published, Chouon published a book called "The Five Seventeen-Article Constitutions," which was included as book 70 of the *Kujiki*-72. Some writers believe that even if parts of the *Kujiki*-72 are forged, these Five Constitutions could be nonetheless authentic.[14] The Five Constitutions are by far the most widely known part of the *Kujiki*-72, so I will explain them in some depth here.

The *Nihon Shoki* ascribes to Prince Shōtoku a single Constitution explaining how officials should behave to ensure peace and prosperity for the nation. It is a remarkable document that demonstrates not only knowledge of Buddhism and Confucianism, but also originality and creativity that allowed the author to play with Chinese concepts and purposefully invent new, more meaningful ways of understanding them. The seventeen articles of this Constitution may be summarized as follows, condensing W. G. Aston's translation:

1. Value harmony and avoid quarreling.
2. Revere the Three Treasures of the Buddha, Dharma, and Sangha.
3. Obey the imperial commands, as Earth obeys Heaven.
4. Ministers must behave with decorum, avoiding attention-seeking and flashy behavior.
5. Deal with public matters as a servant of the law, and avoid bribes and corruption.
6. Chastise evil and reward good. Encourage fidelity among your peers.
7. Take responsibility for your own affairs and do not interfere with the duties of others.
8. Come to work early, and work until late, to ensure that all matters are dealt with.
9. Observe good faith toward both superiors and inferiors.

10. Do not regard yourself as a genius and those around you as fools, but quell your anger and approach others with a calm heart.

11. Ensure that good deeds are rewarded and evil punished.

12. There is only one lord in a country. Do not allow local governors or aristocrats to doubly tax the people.

13. Ensure that all officers report for work and carry out their duty with equal diligence.

14. Do not envy those whose wisdom and genius exceeds yours, but honor them.

15. Turn away from that which is private, and be faithful to that which is public, to prevent resentment and corruption.

16. When the people are at leisure in the winter, press them into service for the state; but when they are busy producing their food and clothing, do not employ them.

17. Decisions on important matters should not be made by one person alone, but by consulting with many.[15]

The striking similarities between the rules laid out in this constitution and how Japanese office workers behave in the twenty-first century should not be called coincidence. Although the Seventeen-Article Constitution is not widely taught in schools, it describes values that have always been shared by public and private officials in Japan, and which may be responsible for Japan's political and economic success.

Note how these articles distinguish the private interests of "the people," which officials must avoid in order to be unbiased judges, from the public interests embodied in the State, which appear to hold some inherent value. Nothing in this document implies that officials are "representatives of the people" or have a "duty" to them. The duties held by officials are toward the State itself, and they are always facing toward it in order to execute their duties with honor and integrity. But why exactly they do this is not defined in the *Nihon Shoki*'s version of this document. The Five Constitutions answer that question.

In the *Kujiki*-72's Five Constitutions, Shōtoku explains that the document summarized above was meant for commoners and was constructed using seventeen essential symbols, which were unknown before the *Kujiki-72*. Furthermore, the Prince gives these essential symbols four all-new interpretations: one each for Buddhists, Confucianists, shrine workers, and politicians, which, including the one for commoners, make a total of five constitutions and eighty-five different articles. The table below gives the general symbols used to construct the five constitutions. These symbols are almost in the same order as the seventeen articles of the *Nihon Shoki* and a comparison will prove useful. The second article, though, has been modified and moved to the end.

PRINCE SHŌTOKU'S 17 SYMBOLS
From book 70 of the *Kujiki-72*[16]

SYMBOL	NAME	EXPLANATION
琴	The Zither	The *koto,* or zither, soothes the heart and calms emotions. Peace requires us to transcend reason and penetrate people's strong emotions. The Zither therefore symbolizes a peaceful heart unfettered by emotional conflict.
斗	The Big Dipper	The motions of the stars follow the laws of the heavens. Therefore the Big Dipper represents superseding human will and bending to Heaven's Law.
月	The Moon	The Moon receives the light of the Sun, and wanes as it retreats from the Sun. The Moon therefore represents knowing one's place in society, knowing when to step back, and revering one's superiors.
臺	The Watchtower	The man in a watchtower must ignore his private needs and selfish desires, and stay vigilant. He has a deep reverence for the concept he protects. The Watchtower is the Way of the Protector.
鏡	The Mirror	The Mirror does not distort but reflects and illuminates all things. Looking in a mirror lets you see something the way it really is. The Mirror is the Way of Enlightenment.
竹	The Bamboo	When arranged side by side, bamboo stalks bear a heavy load. It is chosen because of its strength, and by working selflessly great things will be accomplished. Bamboo is the Way of Service.

SYMBOL	NAME	EXPLANATION
冠	The Cap	Prince Shōtoku instituted a system of 12 ranks, each with its own cap. The Cap means knowing one's strengths and working within one's expertise. The Cap is the Way of Rank.
契	The Covenant	The Covenant is the sacred principle that engenders justice, virtue, and wisdom. The Covenant symbolizes trust in the truth, and is the Way of Truth.
龍	The Dragon	The Chinese dragon is a big creature, but gentle in disposition. Despite the physical power it holds, it is a friend of all the people. The Dragon therefore represents the Way of Humility.
華	The Lotus	The Lotus blossoms beautifully, but its wilting is decreed by Providence. We must understand the natural course that life takes and learn to cope with it. The Lotus is the Way of Things.
日	The Sun	The Sun provides warmth, light, and energy to all without discrimination. All things that happen under Heaven are visible to the Sun above. The leader should act like the Sun and take in all that he can perceive before acting in the interest of all. The Sun is the Way of Leadership.
車	The Carriage	The Carriage is a technology that makes life more efficient, but only if its owner takes care of it. If its wheels go unrepaired it can become more trouble than it's worth. The Carriage is the Way of Sustainability.
地	The Earth	The Earth does not show jealousy toward the heavens, but humbly lies underfoot. It takes virtue to suppress one's self-interest, so the Earth is the Way of Virtue.
天	The Heavens	The Heavens are thought to be above, but really they are all the universe. They are one with everything, so the Heavens are the Way of Non-Self.
水	The Water	Water boils in summer and freezes in winter. It finds a way to make itself useful in all seasons, and takes the shape of whatever vessel it fills. Water is the Way of Utility.

SYMBOL	NAME	EXPLANATION
籠	The Basket	The Basket is marked with gradations so that we might quantify and distinguish what is the larger and the smaller. The Basket is the Way of Goods.
鼎	The Vessel	The Chinese kettle, *kanae,* has three prongs. With fewer than three prongs it cannot stand. Japan, in the same way, has three traditions: Confucianism, Buddhism, and Shinto. All three traditions must be carried on. The Vessel is the Way of the Laws.

Notice how many of these overarching symbols mention disinterest as a virtue, and reject pursuing one's own interests. These ideas may be foreign to us but this is precisely the *organic State* defined by Julius Evola, who proposes that a truly organic State does not produce political parties or factions. Rather, "its representatives, or at least its most qualified ones, should present themselves and rule as some sort of Order, or as a specifically political class, not creating a State within the State, but rather protecting and strengthening the State's key positions; not defending their particular ideology, but rather embodying in an impersonal manner the very pure idea of the State." A copy of the Five Constitutions would have proved heartening to him.[17]

Healthy relations between superior and inferior are also a focus in these articles. This is again precisely as Evola wrote: "Against all forms of resentment and social competition, every person should acknowledge and love his station in life, thus acknowledging the limits within which he can develop his potential; and should give an organic sense to his life and achieve its perfection, since an artisan who perfectly fulfills his function is certainly superior to a king who does not live up to his dignity." It is precisely this attitude, Evola continues, that permitted traditional man to live a life that was materially and spiritually *sustainable.* This is the virtue taught by the Buddhists and other classical philosophers of slowing down and appreciating where you are. He writes:

Progress does not consist in leaving behind one's ranks "to become successful," or in increasing the amount of work in order to gain a position that one is not qualified for. At a higher level, the formula *substine et abstine* ["keep back, but stand firm"] was an axiom of wisdom that echoed through the Classical world; one of the possible interpretations of the Delphic saying "nothing in excess" could also be applied to this order of considerations.[18]

For Evola the stability of tradition comes from remembering these rules, and because the rules are being forgotten we have arrived at our current state of "life out of balance" in both environment and society. The *Kujiki*-72, prescribing the same rules, does not state the consequences of forgetting them, but the early modern period in which it appeared must have felt the glimmering of the same problems.

The fivefold explanations in the Five Constitutions, much lengthier than the short summaries in this table, focus on creating harmony between the different traditions but also extend and deepen the meaning of the original Constitution. I will take just one example, the interesting concept of turning away from the private and toward the public, which the *Kujiki*-72 identifies with the heavens. In the *Nihon Shoki* the corresponding article reads, in full:

> To turn away from that which is private, and to set our faces toward that which is public—this is the path of a Minister. Now if a man is influenced by private motives, he will assuredly feel resentments, and if he is influenced by resentful feelings, he will assuredly fail to act harmoniously with others. If he fails to act harmoniously with others, he will assuredly sacrifice the public interests to his private feelings. When resentment arises, it interferes with order, and is subversive of law. Therefore, in the first clause it was said, that superiors and inferiors should agree together. The purport is the same as this.[19]

The *Kujiki*-72's fourteenth article of the Commoners' Constitution is only slightly different:

To turn away from that which is private, and to set our faces toward that which is public—this is the path of a Minister. Now if a man is influenced by private motives, he will assuredly feel resentments, and if he is influenced by resentments, he will assuredly lose his sincerity. Without sincerity, he will assuredly sacrifice the public interests to his private feelings. When resentment arises, it causes governance to go astray and injures the Law. One must keep the Lord as Lord and governor as governor in one's actions. Therefore when the way of Confucius is defined as *chūsho* 忠恕 in the classics, is this not what we call compassion?[20]

The heavens, according to the *Kujiki-72*'s version, are not really above everything as is commonly thought, but are together with everything. Therefore, to be a truly impartial judge and turn away from private interests, one must discard feelings of selfishness and superiority and adopt a spirit of oneness with those you are responsible for and selfless compassion for their sake alone, which the Confucianists call *chūsho*. This explanation suggests that facing away from private interests and acknowledging superior principles does not mean being cold and uncaring but, on the contrary, could remove our biases and engender true justice. In fact, according to Chouon's disciple Ittei Ishida, compassionate authority might even be thought of as a severe spiritual discipline.[21]

The fourteenth article of the Politicians' Constitution reminds them that the attitude they take toward the public sphere is their attitude toward the world, and essentially toward God. It further informs officials that they are working not to achieve their own ends but for the sake of the king to maintain a working government—a rule today's politicians would do well to heed—and that the king works not for himself but for heaven. Take note of how the world order has fleshed out and become full in this document. The *Nihon Shoki* speaks only of "facing toward the public," but in the *Kujiki-72* the public is recognized as ultimately facing toward the divine, and the king is meant to act out the will of the divinity. "It is necessary," writes Evola, that in a leader "something superhuman and not-human shine forth."[22]

The fourteenth article of the Buddhist Constitution says that Buddha was a saint among saints and the Dharma is a truth among truths, so they should not interpose their personal opinions or try to overexplain the Buddha's message. The article for Shinto shrine workers explains that the nation is built on Sōgen, the rule of heaven, that the important public rites honor the heavenly, earthly, and other ancient kami, and that shrine workers should not allow private individuals to falsely honor suicides and other sorrowful deaths as kami out of the belief that their ghosts will haunt the land if not appeased. Both of these articles seem to concern themselves with preserving traditions and preventing the corruption of private interests.

The fourteenth article of the Confucianists' Constitution, though, is most strange. Instead of a clear explanation of "facing away from what is private" in Confucianism, Shōtoku gives a severe warning to scholars. This is a difficult passage that is translated differently by different authors, but it is worth relating in full.

> Scholars must study the sages of old and should not depend upon the sages of today. Both old histories and recent commentaries record that the sages of old could see the Spirit and knew of the Other World. Accordingly, the people were selfless and did not turn their backs on our kami. Whereas the latter day sages say that Spirit does not exist, have reduced the Other World to water, and have savaged the Soul.* Aah!! And it is not limited to denying of the histories of old! The great Truth that exists in Heaven, the highest aspects of people, the reality of the kami, and the first principles of government are all being violated.[23]

We see here that the Prince Shōtoku of the *Kujiki*-72 seems certain that if the philosophers go back to the earliest and most revered texts,

---

*Ittei Ishida's manuscript at the Saga Prefectural Library appends an alternate reading: "they have lumped the Spirit together with manure, and call the kami emptiness."

they will find original truths there that affirm the existence of Spirit and the Other World. (Certainly if Western philosophers return to the classics, they will find the same message.) Much of the *Kujiki-72* incorporates this metaphysics seamlessly into its narrative, including some sections, like the next, which have had a great impact on Japanese esoterica.

The Hifumi Song and Ten Imperial Treasures

One bit of information unique to the *Kujiki-10*, the version of the *Kujiki* that is generally agreed to have ancient roots, is the "Spell of Furu" or *Hifumi Song*. When Nigihayahi descends to Earth his "heavenly ancestor" (Amaterasu?) sends with him not three but ten heavenly treasures: "one Mirror of the Ocean, one Mirror of the Shore, one Sword of Great Length, one Jewel of Life, one Jewel of Resurrection, one Jewel of the Foot, one Jewel of Return, one Ceremonial Cloth of the [*Orochi*] Serpent, one Ceremonial Cloth of the Bee, and one Ceremonial Cloth of Various Things." Nigihayahi is told that if his earthly body should be pained or those important to him die, he should surround himself with these ten treasures and cry out their numbers, "1 2 3 4 5 6 7 8 9 10," while "swaying back and forth." This will bring the dead to life. A proposed reading for the spell is as follows:[24]

一二三四五六七八九十

Hi fu mi yo i mu na yo ko to

布留部 由良由良 止 布留部

Furube, yurayura to furube

According to the *Kujiki-10*, when Emperor Jimmu conquered Nigihayahi's descendants, he was given these ten treasures, and even in the seventh century CE every November the Hifumi Song was still sung in the court. This is probably the most influential story unique to the *Kujiki-10*. When Atsutane Hirata recounted the story of Amaterasu emerging from the cave, he claimed that this is the song that was sung by Uzume. Furthermore, Hirata said the assignment of these syllables for the numbers one to ten was a later development in Japanese that originally was a sort of chant about the cave meant to get Amaterasu interested.[25]

Several documents from the eighteenth century, found in the archives of the Mononobe clan, describe the esoteric purpose of these treasures and provide illustrations. Each of them is paralleled to one of the five elements and to yin-yang symbolism (fig. 2.4). The significance of the illustrations is unclear today.

So how does the *Kujiki-72* imagine the Hifumi Song? Something like it appears in books 10 and 41, and for some reason this version of the Hifumi Song is well known in esoteric circles. In book 10 the kami Takamimusubi sings a forty-seven-syllable song during the Age of the Kami, and commands it to be used to invent a forty-seven-character script to record the deeds of the kami—that is, kamiyo moji.

棐普味譽彙務奈	夜古堵茂知	爐羅年紫	
Hi fu mi yo i mu na	*Ya ko to mo chi*	*Ro ra ne shi*	

紀流臾闈	厨窊努穌	汚哆坡昫	馬嘉有於
Ki ru yu wi	*Tsu wa nu so*	*O ta ha ku*	*Me ka u wo*

依爾挲	利泪轉	能摩數	亜世會	舗列氣
We ni sa	*Ri he te*	*No ma su*	*A se we*	*Ho re ke*

The *Kujiki-72* explains this verse as follows: The first sixteen syllables are numbers for humans and read "1 2 3 4 5 6 7 8 9 10, 100, 1000, 10,000, 100 million, 1 trillion, 10 quadrillion." Clearly this is no longer related to the Ten Treasures, and the Chinese characters shown above are not even numbers—instead, a translation is supplied afterward. The second sixteen syllables are numerals intended for heaven, and the final fifteen syllables are numbers for Hades. The *Kujiki-72* states that the values of the heaven and hell numbers are not meant to be revealed at this time, but these forty-seven numbers correspond to all forty-seven syllables of modern Japanese, similar to the sentence "the quick brown fox jumps over the lazy dog," which uses all twenty-six English letters.[26]

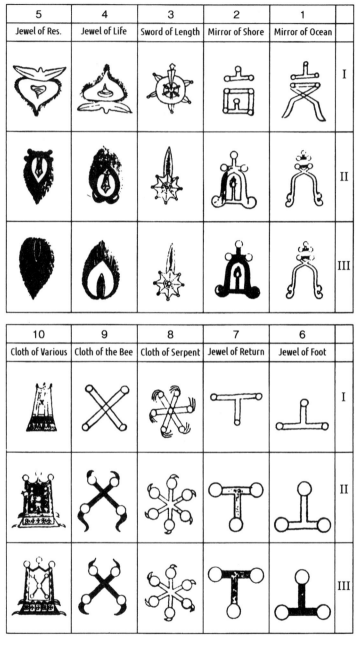

*Figure 2.4. Eighteenth-century illustrations of the Ten Heavenly Treasures.
Note: Japanese is read from right to left as the numbers in this figure reflect.
The Roman numerals along the right side represent versions of each
illustration based on three different manuscripts.
(Courtesy of Shin'ichi Nakaya.)*

When Amaterasu conveys this song to humanity in book 41, another song is included that maps the numbers to a short poem. The key words of this poem (shown as Chinese characters in the original, and capitalized syllables in my transliteration) are the "numbers" from the Hifumi Song, while other syllables are added to fill in the gaps, creating a message for humanity.

人は含む道あり、喜し命報ひ名あり、親と兒は倫の元の因みあり、心は顯れ練り忍へ

Hito ha Fukumu Michi ari Yoshi Inochi Mukuhi Na ari, woYa to Koto ha Tomokara no Moto no Chinami ari, kokoRo ha aRahare Neri Shinohe

There is a Way for humanity, a righteous fame with a happy life, an Original Connection that binds parents to children. Use self-control and temper the passions of the heart.

君は主し豐かに位し、臣は私盗み勿、男は田し畠内草切れ、女は蠶し績織れ

Kimi ha aRushi Yutakani kuraWi shi, yaTsuko ha Watakushi Nusumi seSo, Otoko ha Takaya shi Hatauchi Kusakire, Me ha Kokahi shi Umi Wore

Kings should rule gently, and their officials must not steal for themselves. Men, tend to your paddies and till your fields. Women, spin clothing from the cocoons of the silkworms.

家は饒ひ榮やせ、理は宜に照らせ、法は守り進め、悪きなきことは攻絶め、欲みと我をは刪れ

iWe ha Nikihahi Sakayase, kotowaRi ha muHe ni Terase Nori ha Mamori Susume, Achiki naki koto ha Semeta Weshime, Hoshimi to aRe wo ha Ketsure

Let the households flourish and prosper! Shine the light of the Truth on all! Keep and fulfill the Law! Defeat evil, and eliminate every selfish desire![27]

Some of the crucial lessons of the Five Constitutions are repeated here. The first line of the poem exhorts all people to follow the Way to thoughtfulness and compassion. In the second line each person is given a role to play in society and a general reminder of how to execute this role. Finally, Amaterasu admonishes humanity to stay on the right path to ensure happiness and prosperity.

The forty-seven-syllable song has strong esoteric meanings of unknown age that carry on today. It is the basis of *chinkon-kishin,* a Shinto form of meditation that can be practiced by anyone and is chanted at the beginning of a meditation session. It is also considered the song of creation by some Shinto traditions and can sometimes be found on the wall of an esoteric training room written in kamiyo moji. Where exactly did the author of the *Kujiki*-72, whether he was medieval or ancient, get this secret information? Did he invent it, hear it from a teacher, or see it in a text?

The "last national scholar," Yoshio Yamada, proposed in 1953 that this incantation was invented for the *Kujiki*-72. He claimed it could not be ancient because it contains all forty-seven syllables of spoken Japanese, and the Japanese supposedly had no knowledge of syllables before Chinese writing was imported and probably spoke a very different language. But the critic Minoru Harada has recently challenged this theory: If these verses are original to the *Kujiki*-72, how on Earth did they become so influential throughout the Shinto world? In the opinion of Shintoists the Hifumi Song was considered too sacred to record before the *Kujiki*-72 but has existed for many centuries. Furthermore there is linguistic evidence that the verses of Amaterasu's song are written in Old Japanese, using grammar so subtle that early modern commentators did not understand it. But if the ancients understood the syllabic nature of language, what does that mean about kamiyo moji?[28]

What is clear is that this later Hifumi Song appeared in a completely different era from the tenth-century version, and it seems to have matched some inexplicable desire for a more relevant song. Other parahistories provide their own, competing Hifumi songs to match their alternative images of Japan. The idea of a song of origin seems to have resonated with Japanese people both then and now.

THE *KUJIKI'S* LEGACY
AND THE *HITSUKI SHINJI*

The *Kujiki-*72 was probably the first parahistory, but is it the birth of a genre? It seems to me it could have provided some of the inspiration for Norinaga Motoori's work with the *Kojiki,* but the link to other parahistories is more tenuous. As we will see, none of the four documents I have chosen are really anything like each other. Generally the *Kujiki-*72 is responsible for a great number of new ideas. Even while it was banned it was secretly consulted by national scholars like Zankō Masuho, and in the twentieth century when it was rediscovered it seems to have inspired someone, or something.[29]

When the *Kujiki* was unbanned in the imperial period, many independent researchers studied and promoted it. Generally they were interested in promoting a patriotic interest in Japan's heritage, but a few of these researchers took parahistory into a totally different realm. In April 1944 a meeting of parahistorians carried out an unusual kind of ancient Chinese divination, using branches in sand to spell out letters. Rather than giving expected answers like a Ouija board, though, when the parahistorians asked who they were speaking to, the branches spelled out the characters Ame, Hi, Tsu, Ku 天ヒツク, which meant absolutely nothing to anyone present. Perhaps some trickster spirit had interfered with the process.

The parahistorians were roundly disappointed, except for a man named Tenmei Okamoto who felt somehow intrigued. He went to an encyclopedia of shrines and looked up the unknown name, discovering that there was a shrine with that name not too far from Tokyo. When he visited this shrine, his arm began to throb with pain, and he was suddenly possessed to take up a brush and start writing. He looked down at the paper and discovered that he was unable to read what he had written. This was the beginning of the *Hitsuki Shinji* (fig. 2.5), the "Sun-Moon Revelation," a collection of 100 books of automatic writing in a unique script replete with phonetic numbers and other symbols (much like Christian mystic Emanuel Swedenborg's "writings from

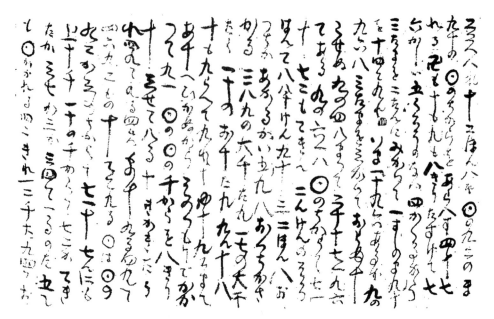

Figure 2.5. Detail from the Hitsuki Shinji *manuscript.*

heaven made up of mere numbers"), which could be deciphered only slowly and with agony.

The *Hitsuki Shinji,* which has not yet been rendered properly in English, claims to be written by the God of Abraham, Christ, and Mohammed. The first chapters written in 1944 forecast that Japan would lose World War II, but rebuild quickly. This manuscript was widely copied in the Japanese Army and is said to have saved some despairing officers from suicide in 1945. The following chapters deal with what would come after that rebuilding: God warns that the modern world is unsustainable and has been misguided by occult forces, called "Ishiya" (masons?), which are leading it straight to collapse. What is coming within our lifetimes, according to proponents of the *Hitsuki Shinji,* is a worldwide crisis that will be as precipitious as walking along the edge of a cliff, but human beings will be able to pull through this challenge by growing a spiritual resilience. It asserts that "all things will become one-third" of their former sizes, which seems to imply a great reduction in arable land, food, and population.

In the *Hitsuki Shinji* Japan is Nihon, the "Nation of Origin," and in the coming crisis those loyal to Nihon will have a unique challenge to face that requires special spiritual training. The symbol for Origin used in the text is Ⓢ, which kotodama experts may be familiar with as the symbol for "Su," divine consciousness. Much of the book is concerned with instructing the people of the Nation of Ⓢ in finding the original "crystal" nature of their souls as a portion of kami, and directing them toward becoming one with kami.

This would seem to make the *Hitsuki Shinji* a text relevant primarily to people born in Japan. But surprisingly, from its very first book, the *Shinji* asserts that it is not speaking of a political nation but of a spiritual one: "Some are loyal to foreign lands even in the nation of Ⓢ, and some are children of kami even in foreign lands." In other words, to adhere to the way of the kami is to be a member of the nation of Nihon, but this is not the same as being physically born in Japan, and indeed, even a Japanese citizen may be spiritually a member of another nation.

The *Hitsuki Shinji* makes reference to the philosophy of the *Kujiki*-72 in some places and gives a name for the Creator Kami that more closely resembles the *Kujiki*-72 than the *Kujiki*-10. It also tells us that "The Five of Heaven reveals itself on Earth as the Five Weights," and lists those Five Weights in order. And it quotes the forty-seven-syllable Hifumi Song. Whatever that historical current was that Chouon had caught on to, it appears that the author of the *Hitsuki Shinji* likes it as well.

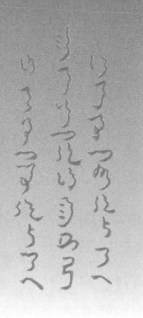

3
Finnegan's Waka

The *Hotsuma Tsutaye* and Woshite Corpus

In 1966 there were many exciting things to see in Tokyo. You could marvel at the imposing steel of Tokyo Tower, see the hottest fashions in Shinjuku and Ginza, or visit the brand-new stadium where the Olympics had just been held. Or, if you were Yoshinosuke Matsumoto (1919–2003), you could descend into the dusty bowels of a used bookstore in the old academic quarter. There, hidden among medieval occult texts and grimoires, the amateur philologist stumbled upon a fragmentary manuscript with the unreadable title

Ⅲ ⌁ ⊕ ⌁ ⊘ ⚹

Matsumoto took this curiosity home with him with some other prewar books he had rescued from the store. The other books proved of little interest. But the book with the unreadable title was something much greater. Like the title, the contents were written in a strange, unknown script. It appeared to be linked to Japanese, and it had a regular meter. After only a few hours of work, Matsumoto figured out that he now possessed an unknown epic poem entitled *Hotsuma Tsutaye,* a history of the earliest eras of Japan.

Having read the *Nihon Shoki* and *Kojiki,* as well as parallel texts like the Old Testament, we would expect the first lines of this poem to tell of the creation of the universe. But in this book the beginning is *not* the beginning. Instead, we begin by reading about the life of a single woman and the royal circumstances of her upbringing.

sore waka wa — Waka hime no kami

suterarete — hirota to sodatsu

Kanasaki no — tsuma no chi o yete

awa uwa ya — tefuchi shiho no me

As for that *waka:* Kami Princess Waka,
abandoned, is now found and raised.
From the wife of Kan'saki she taketh her milk,
babbling *awa, uwa,* hands clapping, bright eyes.

Like Moses, Romulus, and Remus, Waka is an abandoned child destined for greatness. But what country is this? Where, and when, are we? Rather than clarifying directly, the text launches into a list of ceremonies for children in ancient Japan and lessons that parents teach their children.

umare hi wa — kashi mike sonahe

tachi mahi ya — mi fuyu kami oki

hatsu hi mochi — awa no uyamahi

On the morrow of birth, offer rice with red beans
and dance *tachi mahi.* Bundle hair at third winter.
Come New Year, eat *mochi,* and offer the prayers to Heaven
and Earth.[1]

At this point we might realize with a shock why the text has begun with the birth of a single child. The *Hotsuma Tsutaye* has a task even more formidable than explaining the origin of the universe: it is trying to educate us about what life was like in the age of the kami, a subject missing completely from the official histories. Indeed, resurrecting this forgotten age for its readers is the perfect goal for a text written in a forgotten script.

Only after we pass through a child's education do we learn that Princess Waka was the inventor of the 5–7–5–7 waka meter this epic poem follows. Next we learn of her romantic troubles in adulthood and begin to understand the lives, loves, and trials of the ancient Hotsuma kingdom. We learn how Waka, after being abandoned by her parents as a bad luck child, was later happily reunited with them. This, rather than the creation of the heavens and the Earth, is the story that the *Hotsuma Tsutaye* wants to tell first.*

After years of study Matsumoto concluded that the phrase "as for that waka" is not meant to be a complete sentence.[3] Rather, this poem of over 10,000 regular lines begins in the middle of a sentence and spirals outward, like *Finnegan's Wake.* And, as in the *Wake,* many of the words in the *Hotsuma Tsutaye* are not known to us from any extant language and cannot be easily comprehended. But the text claims to date to the 100s CE, and sings of arms and the man, and of the accomplishments of great people of that primeval era.

Matsumoto's fragment was printed in the nineteenth century and it would be reasonable to assume that some modern eccentric with knowl-

---

*Waka was found, that is, *hirota,* and raised into a princess who wrote beautiful songs. Today Hirota Shrine in Hyogo prefecture is well known to have a tradition of waka music, going back to before recorded history.[2]

edge of Western epics, ancient literature, the Ainu people of northern and central Japan, and traditional symbolism might have put it together. Yet, as research continued on the *Hotsuma Tsutaye,* manuscripts were found from as early as 1777, and other texts from this corpus dated to 1764 or earlier. I couldn't believe my eyes when I saw this fact. In that century even the most educated Japanese could have known nothing about epic poetry or Ainu culture. Even if it was forged at that time, this is quite an important achievement in world literature—the first Japanese epic poem (by several centuries), the first poem written in a constructed language (again by several centuries), and so forth. Whoever wrote this was either a godlike individual who had the ability to invent entire genres of literature in his head or an initiate passing on an even more extraordinary ancient tradition.

Can there be any doubt of the aesthetic value of this masterpiece? Could that, by itself, serve as evidence that we are looking at the lost remnants of a great preclassical civilization? We must give some credence to the parahistorians who write that the *Hotsuma Tsutaye* "has ancientness to it which one can sense in between its beautiful words. There are many words missing from even the largest dictionaries of ancient language, and the language carries a beautiful melody. This sense is not associated with fakery."[4]

A LOST EPIC SECRETLY PRESERVED

After explaining the Hotsuma educational system and the origins of its own poetic meter, the *Hotsuma Tsutaye* narrative matures into a sophisticated overview of ancient Japan. The early chapters deal with the age of the kami, vaguely akin to the *Kojiki* and *Nihon Shoki,* but in the *Hotsuma Tsutaye* the kami are not immaterial beings but rather a race of powerful, semi-immortal nobles who descended from the north. In these early chapters the kami are often sitting around in the court relating stories of earlier times, like in the Socratic dialogues. Actually, they are often asking each other questions about language and the symbolism of the nation, which provide an opening to launch into long stories.

The preface explains that the first half of the *Hotsuma Tsutaye* was originally an epic recitation, like the *Iliad*. (Also like the *Iliad* the characters are given epithets, called *tatahena*.) Researchers have gleaned from the text that the Japanese of that era did not know how to make paper but were able to make temporary pedagogical markings, called *woshite* ✪ 𠕋 𠔻, on cloth using mulberry dye (fig. 3.1). These were used for conveying messages and official pronouncements, and there was a method of education and scribes, but the medium of dye was impermanent and washed away. Although the word woshite is unknown in modern Japanese, in the *Nihon Shoki* the word *oshide* meaning "seal" does appear, and even today some Shinto shrines used to hold writings from the imperial court are called *Oshide-sha*.[5]

In the prehistoric kingdom where it was produced, the *Hotsuma* song was well loved and constantly sung for centuries, with no danger of being forgotten, just like the status of the *Iliad* among the prehistoric Greeks. Around the first century CE, however, signs of decay were showing. Boat after boat of immigrants arrived from the west with their own stories and beliefs. The seven native clans, seeking proof of their authority, were fabricating their own historical records, which made them out to be the most important, just as Prince Shōtoku later lamented in the *Kujiki*-72. The harried Emperor Woshirowake asked the imperial scribe Ohotataneko to continue the

Figure 3.1. The woshite syllabary.
Note how consonants and vowels match together to form characters.

old *Hotsuma* narrative to the present day and make a complete manuscript of it.

Ohotataneko fulfilled his duty and presented the finished document to the court in 126 CE. It contained twenty-eight aya (chapters) revised from the original and twelve aya composed by Ohotataneko himself. In his additions we learn that around the time of the ancient Greeks, Japan developed a sort of constitutional monarchy ruled by an emperor called *amakimi* ☉ ♀ Ⅱ 兀. The *amakimi* was responsible for understanding the hearts of the people and building a country that would allow them to achieve their natural destinies.

Parahistorians believe that Emperor Woshirowake may have been the last to use woshite, since in his era a good one-third of inhabitants of Japan were recent immigrants, bringing new technology and knowledge with them from the mainland. Some parts of the Hotsuma legends were still in oral circulation, but the full poem was no longer extant. The stray quotes were merged with local legends and oral genealogies of the imperial family, and the mishmash that resulted gave birth to the rather unpoetic *Kojiki, Kujiki,* and *Nihon Shoki*. There were great fights over what the correct history was. Various clans demanded that the imperial family recognize the superiority of their ancestral kami and backed their words with swords drawn. Entire lineages suffered and died over questions of theology and history. When the last elders who could make the woshite dyes passed from this world, it was completely forgotten.

Provenance of the Extant Woshite Corpus

Like the rongorongo of Easter Island, much of the woshite corpus is destroyed today, but fragments of the *Hotsuma Tsutaye* and other documents have been found in various places, together constituting three verified texts. Unfortunately, when these manuscripts were recovered in early modern times, scholars shunned the idea of texts from the age of the kami, casting them into the world of parahistory.

The *Hotsuma Tsutaye* is the most complete woshite text, handed down from Ohotataneko through the Waniko family. A register of families from 815 tells us that the Waniko household is descended from Lord Atakatasu, who the *Kujiki*-10 tells us was the father of Ohotataneko. In the final aya the poem tells us that it was deposited in a treasure house at the Shrine of A-Wa—apparently the same place where the *Kujiki*-72's source text was discovered. Other than this, we know little about how it survived the centuries.[6]

In the 1700s the last male Waniko died, entrusting the manuscript to his grandson Yūnoshin Ibo. Ibo accepted the manuscript as a treasure, deciphered it, and painstakingly translated it into Classical Chinese over a period of thirty years. In 1775 he presented the finished product (fig. 3.2) to the Emperor, hoping that his translation and commentary could allow scholars to consider the text seriously. As far as we know he worked completely alone in rural Shiga prefecture and there are no records that anyone else helped him with his translation. He gives his name as "Yasutoshi Waniko" in the document, a symbol of his lifelong devotion to his inheritance.[7]

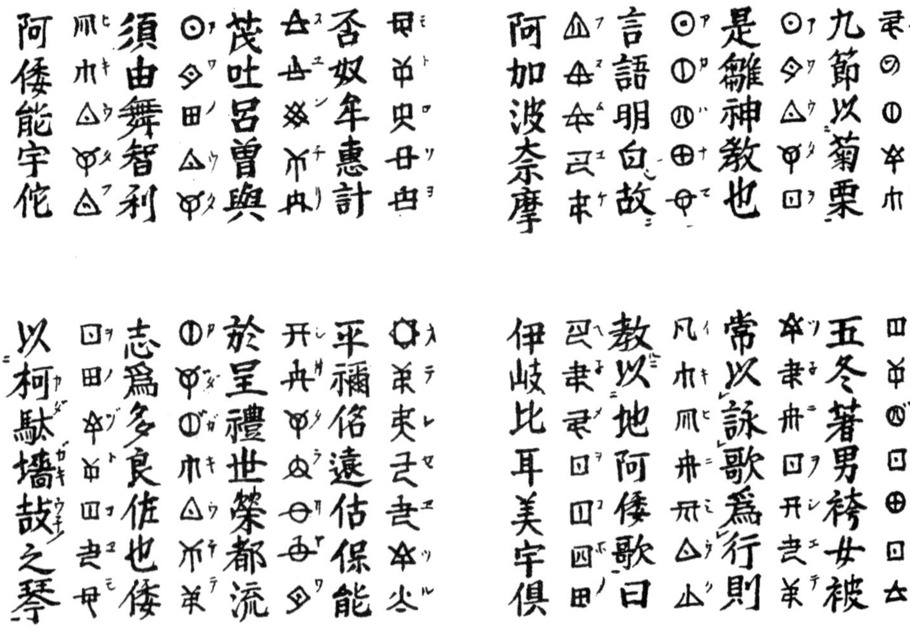

Figure 3.2. A sample manuscript page of Yūnoshin Ibo's 1775 edition of the Hotsuma Tsutaye *with Chinese characters alongside woshite.*

By 1775, though, Japan's scholars were fully engaged deciphering the chaotic mixture of legends and genealogy in the *Nihon Shoki* and *Kojiki* into a single, coherent message that could justify a more coherent political regime than the corrupt shogunate. A few decades earlier the Mitogaku school had purposefully omitted the age of the kami in its *Great History of Japan* (Dainihonshi) since it was a topic of endless speculation with little modern, political relevance. The scholarly Mitogaku history begins precisely where the *Hotsuma Tsutaye* ends.[8]

Just a few years before, in the 1760s, the influential Kokugaku school had begun a great revisionist project to promote the *Kojiki* over the *Nihon Shoki,* but the *Hotsuma Tsutaye* seemed to endorse the *Nihon Shoki* as the earlier text. It was really the worst possible scholarly environment for the *Hotsuma Tsutaye* to appear in, so other than attracting the idle interest of a few Buddhist monks and other independent esotericists, it was completely ignored. Atsutane Hirata, finding it uninteresting, left us an irritatingly short, but intriguing description: "These are the Clay Urn Hotsuma Letters. We hear that a book with these letters exists in the Shrine of A-Wa, placed there by Ohotataneko. These Hotsuma Letters may also be seen in the treasure house of Ise Jingū."[9] Ibo's 1775 manuscript was found in a shrine in 1992 and is the earliest record we have of the *Hotsuma Tsutaye*. The search for earlier manuscripts continues.

The *Mikasafumi* 帯 ① ⊖ ⚞ 帯, a text written by a Minister of the Left in the Yayoi period, also survives in small fragments. Eight parts of a total sixty-four were found in a nineteenth-century copy, and one more part was found in the papers of the Buddhist monk Fusen— dating, significantly, to 1764, over a decade before the first manuscript of the *Hotsuma Tsutaye* appeared. The excerpts describe annual festivals and imperial rites, and thus the *Mikasafumi* appears to be similar in form to the official Engishiki, a fifty-volume book about laws and customs completed in 927 CE.[10]

The last surviving work is the *Futomani* ⚞ 中 中 帯, a manuscript for divination according to the rules set out by the *Hotsuma Tsutaye* and *Mikasafumi,* allegedly written by Amaterasu and understood to be an esoteric text, which will only impart an outer, superficial meaning to non-initiates. It was widely referenced by Buddhist monks in the Edo period, but our only extant manuscript of it is held by the prestigious Ogasawara family. They keep it in their treasure house and do not generally exhibit it. A copy, made by Kuniyoshi Nogai from 1914 to 1922, is now available to the public. These three documents are the only ones known to researchers.*

Rediscovering the Text

When Matsumoto discovered his fragment in 1966, the text quoted in it was completely unknown to history. Other than that fragment, nobody had ever discussed it in a printed publication. In fact, nobody knew where the complete copy could be found. So he took the only information he had—a couple of names written on the front of the transcription—and set out into unfamiliar corners of Japan seeking any descendants of those unknown names. Everywhere he went he found dead ends: a demolished shrine, an extinct family, a memory of a worm-eaten manuscript burnt in honor of the ancestors. When he finally found a complete edition, it was, as far as we know, one of only two complete copies that existed in the world at that time. He rushed home to transcribe it, clutching it like a treasure.

As he tried to make sense of what he had found, Matsumoto acquired copies of the *Kojiki* and *Nihon Shoki* and began comparing the respective stories, and soon his study was filled with notes. He could not handle the workload on his own, so he recruited fellow researchers who worked sleepless nights putting together concordances and chronologies. Every month new parallels were discovered between the text and old documents and shrines, and the *Hotsuma*

---

*But are there more in the Ise Jingū archives? One woshite researcher has reported that a number of woshite texts were discovered in a windowless, doorless room in a very old household in Fukushima prefecture while it was being dismantled in 1967. The owner of the house reported that he had sold the texts to Ise Jingū, which keeps many of its collections secret, such as the extra ten books of the *Kujiki*-31. (See *Hotsuma* newsletter, November 1996.)

Tsutaye became Matsumoto's driving passion for the rest of his life. In a remarkable passage he describes the experience as follows:

> As my study of the Hotsuma Tsutae has progressed, I have noticed a curious transformation in my awareness. Before my discovery, Amaterasu, Yamatotake, Isanagi and the rest were objects of a dim sensation of awe—ivory-carved "gods" existing on some fluffy white cloud of reverence and sanctity. And, as such, faceless.
>
> Now, I feel I have come to know these characters as real people who lived, loved, suffered, and died. Rejoiced, grieved, pondered, and wondered. In a word, they have become human, thanks to the Hotsuma Tsutae.[11]

Matsumoto tried to alert the academic world to his discovery but he was met with stony silence, and to this day not a single academic has considered the matter. No journal or conference has ever accepted any paper that mentions it. Matsumoto was forced to go to the newspapers, which gave him some coverage, but without official approval the text can have no impact on Japan's public sphere. Commendably, Matsumoto treated the woshite corpus with scholarly integrity and respect, never making any attempt to claim ownership of it or conceal his work from others. His work lives on in several excellent critical editions of the text available at large libraries across Japan.

Throughout his travels Matsumoto was unable to find any record of what had happened to the original woshite manuscripts preserved by Yūnoshin Ibo. For over twenty years Matsumoto and his fellow researchers put out the word about the *Hotsuma Tsutaye,* asking amateur historians to check the treasure houses of their neighborhood shrines for unusual manuscripts. Finally, in 1992, a man named Takao Ibo found the original Ibo manuscript in a shrine near his home, rediscovering the original epic poem 320 years after it was transcribed. It must be noted that woshite researchers did the genealogy and discovered that this Takao Ibo was the great-great-great-great-great-grandson of Yūnoshin.

Woshite, a Language of Symbolism

The most spectacular difference between the earlier *Kujiki*-72 and the *Hotsuma Tsutaye* is its script, called woshite. This script, like medieval and modern Japanese, contains forty-eight syllables and five distinct vowels. Unlike ordinary Japanese script, though, the symbols were created with a regular system. The vowel markers combine with consonant markers to create a glyph. In the poem the script is put to countless uses for kotodama and other revelatory purposes, and I will try to cover just a few here.

Matsumoto did much of the work discovering evidence of the *Hotsuma Tsutaye*'s authenticity in the names of shrines and kami scattered across Japan. He places great importance on the Song of A and Wa ⊚ ⊚ ⊞ △ ⑦, a two-person didactic theme, which recurs throughout the poem from Princess Waka to the end. Like the Hifumi Song, this song uses all forty-eight syllables of woshite, arranged in a phonetic order:

a ka ha na ma   i ki hi ni mi u ku

hu nu mu e ke   he ne me o ko ho no

mo to ro so yo   wo te re se ye tsu ru

su yu n chi ri   shi yi ta ra sa ya wa

Note that the *a* ⊚, at the beginning of this song, and the *wa* ⊚, at the end, are not the ordinary woshite syllables, but left-turning and right-turning spirals, representing heaven and Earth, male and female, yang and yin. In the third aya we learn that when Izanagi and Izanami go around the pillar together, part of their ritual involves singing this song. The first twenty-four characters belong to male Izanagi, who begins the song while "turning to the left" (⊙ ⊕ ⋒ ⑦ ⋔ *wo wa hidari*).

The second twenty-four characters belong to the female Izanami, who ends the song while "turning to the right" (吞 ⦿ 开 爪 吞 厶 舟 *me wa migi meguri*). If we write this song in lines of five syllables, we discover that it becomes a syllabary, with the two halves fitting together to show the inner logic of woshite. According to the fifth aya, "By singing the Song of A and Wa, the voice became clearer and speech was improved. The corrupted language corrected itself, order returned to the land, and peace reigned once more." This must be why the song was one of the first things taught to Princess Waka.[12]

The well-known artist Rei Torii, who finds inspiration for his art in the *Hotsuma Tsutaye,* does not focus on the Song of A and Wa or the Ame-no-Michi, but rather on the Five Elements it describes: Space, Wind, Fire, Water, and Stone. These correspond to the five vowel sounds of woshite as follows:

⊙   A—Space (yang)
ⴄ   I—Wind (yang)
△   U—Fire (yang)
ꋬ   E—Water (yin)
▣   O—Stone (yin)

In Japan these are known as the five great elements 五大. Because they were used in medieval Buddhist esotericism it is believed they were brought to Japan from India, but in fact they do not correspond to any Indian text, and the *Hotsuma Tsutaye* demonstrates that they are a native doctrine of this country. Everything in the universe is made from combinations of these five elements, but only one being is made from the union of all five: man.[13]

Mitsuru Ikeda, who has done the most serious research since Matsumoto's death, is interested in the text's concepts of government and righteousness. The overarching principle of the woshite universe is called *to-no-woshite* 中 田 ✿ 开 羊, implying that to know, and to understand writing and books, is to rule. This unwritten law manifests itself as the Way of Heavenly Being, *Ame-naru-Michi,* which changes from era to era and makes different demands of different people. For statesmen there is a proper way to rule, and for ordinary people of the nation there are norms that should be protected. The nation is defined through these ways, and preserving them takes precedence over political bickering.[14]

Seiji Takabatake of the Japan Translation Center has an interest in ancient futomani divination, described in chapter 1. The woshite book of Futomani has a fascinating chart that shows fifty-one glyphs arranged in a circular pattern (fig. 3.3). These fifty-one glyphs are all different outcomes for the divination. At the center the symbols ⊚, ᚂ, ◎ represent the Creator and origin. The inner ring of eight glyphs surrounding it show the eight heavenly kami; the middle ring contains the eight kami governing the eight compass directions, language, and the body; and the thirty-two glyphs in the two outer rings represent outer manifestations. Unfortunately, nowhere in the woshite corpus do we find a description of how to perform this divination. If anyone has this information, such as the house of Ogasawara, they are keeping it secret.

Finally, I would be remiss to overlook Andrew Driver, an Englishman who has worked with Takabatake for many years and has already translated several books about the *Hotsuma Tsutaye*. In Driver's current studies he has taken a look at the Hotsuma culture's concept of the afterlife as expressed by the unusual word *tamakaeshi* ☿ ☖ ① ᘔ ᚩ, which seems to express a belief that the human soul, called orb or tama, belongs in another world but has been bound to a physical body, *shiyii* ᚩ ᚩ, and will be released at death and "returned" (*kaeshi*) to its place of origin, perhaps finding another body to inhabit. This belief does not appear in the *Nihon Shoki* and *Kojiki*, which were both produced centuries after the arrival of Buddhism in Japan, and mainstream Shinto does not know of it, but the word *tama-shii* survives in ancient and modern Japanese—only its deeper meaning has been forgotten. Furthermore, this doctrine of tamakaeshi (souls "returning to origin") is taught in Shinto-based new religions like Tenrikyo.

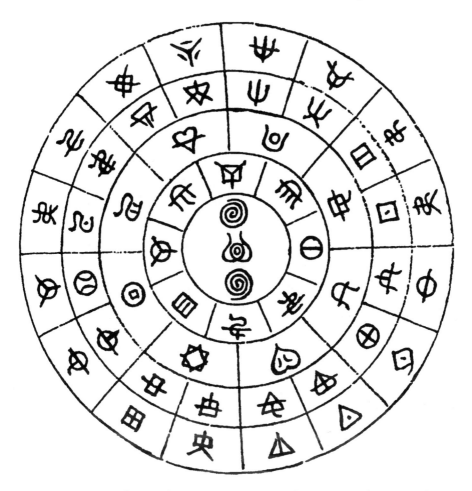

Figure 3.3. According to the Hotsuma Tsutaye, *this futomani divination chart was used in ultra-ancient times to predict the course of the future.*

According to the *Hotsuma Tsutaye,* when a child is born a part of God descends to Earth. This inner seed of God is cut off from God but is still the same substance in the way that a child is still part of her mother after the umbilical cord is cut.[15]

The *Hotsuma Tsutaye's* view of the afterlife is unusual in medieval Japan, and I look forward to Driver's forthcoming book, tentatively entitled *Echoes of Antiquity,* which will touch on this and other subjects, examining the case for the *Hotsuma Tsutaye's* antiquity in full.

THE HEAVENLY LORD
OF ULTRA-ANCIENT JAPAN

Now it is my turn to tell the Hotsuma story. Lacking the space to properly cover everything, I will limit myself to discussing the life and teachings of Amaterasu, not the only character in the narrative but one who plays a prominent role. Those seeking more can look online for copies of *The World of the Hotsuma Legends* (1996) and *The Hotsuma Legends: Paths of the Ancestors* (1999), translated by Andrew Driver and published by the Japan Translation Center in Tokyo.

Over the course of this poem we realize that Lord Amaterasu ⊙ ⊕ ⼇ ⍉ △, who is more often called Amateru ⊙ ⊕ ⼇ ⼂, was not just a kami out there in space but was a real ruler of Japan who, like Lord Rama in the Hindu epics, was faced with difficult decisions and responded with courage and compassion. Lord Amateru's honorable noblesse oblige is a far cry from the strange figure of the *Kojiki* who does not appear to be much of a leader, and Mitsuru Ikeda feels that by reading the *Hotsuma Tsutaye* "we become able to respect Amateru as a teacher for our lives, and to follow his example."

In this story Lord Amateru is in fact male. This is not an anomaly; many medieval scholars at the time of the *Hotsuma Tsutaye*'s 1777 presentation to the imperial court considered the concept of a "Sun Goddess" a mismatch of traditional symbolism and were propounding that Amateru must have originally been male.[16] Julius Evola, working from the very limited and poorly translated material available to him, also believed a female Amateru to be "a confusing transposition of the feminine principle."[17] According to woshite researchers his instinct was correct, since the record has been confused.

When we compare stories we find that records of Lord Amateru's sister Princess Waka in the *Hotsuma Tsutaye* have been rewritten to pertain to Amateru in the *Nihon Shoki*. Woshite researchers believe that Amateru, having been forgotten and reduced to a name during the Himiko/Yamatai era like so many of the kami, was recast as female hundreds of years later. Yoshinosuke Matsumoto believed that

these changes were originally made in Prince Shōtoku's *Kujiki* to create a justification for female imperial succession—Amateru does appear
as female in both the *Kujiki*-10 and *Kujiki*-72. Actually, a medieval
scholar named Nobutsune Watarai found evidence in the most ancient
records at Ise Jingū that Amateru could have originally been male, since
the kami was associated with male clothing long before the first histories were written. Furthermore, circumstancial evidence suggests that
esoteric Buddhist sects had knowledge of Amateru's real identity even
as late as the medieval period.[18]

Lord Amateru is the "Kami of the Sun," born to Izanami and
Izanagi in a golden age described as thousands of years before the
present day. This is all vaguely similar to the official histories. In the
Hotsuma Tsutaye, though, we learn that after his birth Lord Amateru
is taken to a palace and given his first bath by Izanagi's sister, Princess
Shirayama. There are more than 2,600 shrines in Japan dedicated to
Shirayama, but one would be hard pressed to find any reference to
her in the official histories. This seems to evidence that the *Hotsuma
Tsutaye* conveys some knowledge not found in these histories.[19]

Amateru's Education

When he was sixteen Amateru and his cousin were sent to live with
Izanagi's father Toyoke 中 卪 串 to study the meaning of life and
the principles of right government. This required moving to Toyoke's
home in Takamagahara/Hitakami, the original abode of the gods.
Woshite researchers identify this Hitakami 爪 Ｙ Ф 丗 with the
coast of Tohoku (northern Japan), where they say there was an ancient
kingdom. But the name Hitakami actually means "vision of a high sun"
and the fourth aya describes it as a place "where the sun rises high." It
seems to me that this Hitakami could easily have been farther north
than Tohoku.

Amateru's teacher mixes a doctrine of right and benevolent government with an understanding of rebirth. People's past lives, he
says, determine what role they will be born into in their present life.
Understanding that you are living out the consequences of your past

actions can help you to accept your position in life. With these lessons Amateru realizes the importance of a calm mind. This teaching is called the Way of Heavenly Being, *Ame-naru-Michi*.[20]

Returning from Hitakami with knowledge of the first principles of government and happy living, Amateru becomes the *amakami* ☉ ♀ ◑ 爪, or Heavenly Lord, of the Hotsuma kingdom. His reign is long and peaceful, and the people are deeply grateful. But it is not without its treacherous moments.

Susanowo and the Rock Cave

In this poem, as in the official histories, Amateru hides in a rock cave to avoid brother Susanowo. But the *Hotsuma Tsutaye*'s Susanowo is a little different. His myth cycle is not tied into Izumo, but rather with Kumano, south of Ise. Susanowo is a rotten child as in the official story and his mother Izanami, ashamed at her son's defilement, builds the Kumano Shrines in the wilderness to atone for her mistakes. Susanowo stupidly starts a forest fire and burns his mother with the shrines (note how her death is by an otherwise unknown "fire kami" in the *Kojiki*), which explains why these shrines have been a center of pilgrimage throughout Japanese history despite lack of any discussion of them in the official histories. Izanagi then looks upon his wife's rotting body against warnings, is chased away by demon spirits, and has to fight them off with peaches.[21]

Later Susanowo goes on another rage, indirectly killing one of Lord Amateru's wives. This parallels the events of the official histories, but here Amateru does not attempt to rectify the situation by reinterpreting his brother's deeds. Instead he tries to teach him a lesson in the basics of the *Ame-naru-Michi:*

Ame ga shita   yawashite meguru

Hi tsuki koso   harete akaruki

☿ ⊼ 田 ☿ ⚮ ⊕ ⊼

Tami no tara nari

Just as the sun and moon navigate the heavens,
Become a parent to the world, shining down on those below.

But again Susanowo does not take kindly to these gentle words, and Amateru hides in a cave, casting the world into darkness. His ministers convene and set up a shamanistic session outside the cave. As in the *Kojiki* a group of women named Uzume attract Amateru's curiosity with a song and dance, although no nudity is mentioned here.[22]

After Amateru is restored to his throne, a punishment must be decided for Susanowo. The court decides that only the death penalty could be suitable for such wanton destruction. But one of the ministers appeals to the court's sense of mercy, and after consulations Susanowo is sent on his way with a warning that his problems stemmed from being born under a bad moon.

The remarkable thing about the rock cave story in this narrative is that it's included at all. Lord Amateru has so many other matters of state to handle and teachings to disperse that the problem of his unruly brother seems a little out of place. Specifically, he must conquer the biggest uprising Japan had ever seen: the *hatare*.

HOW LORD AMATERU SAVED JAPAN

Even the greatest hero of his age, apparently, cannot create total law and order throughout the land. One year, Lord Amateru receives word from the regional governments that many tribes are being manipulated by disaffected people, the hatare, and are rising up in a great rebellion. The hatare use black magic to trick their followers into disobeying the Way of Heaven and are causing much suffering and starvation among ordinary people. There are six groups of hatare, totaling over 700,000 rebels, all over the land. Considering that the Hotsuma kingdom had only five million households, this clearly meant that government could no longer function.[23]

Amateru's court is totally unprepared for this, and with their own forces numbering only 800, swift and decisive action is needed. Some of his advisors call for a policy of no mercy—death to the hatare and anyone who harbors them—but the amakami silences these angry words. Instead, he says, the court must focus on the anger that burns inside them, consuming their hearts, for in this anger exists a subtle truth about their nature.

Yaya shiru makoto:

Hatare to ha

ame ni mo orasu

kami narasu

hito no nechike wo

tokisukure

koriyete mutsu no

hatare nari

At last, here is the truth:
What are the hatare? They exist not in heaven,
nor are they kami. They seize on and sharpen
the deviance of men, driving them to blindness.
These are the six hatare.

In other words, having examined their behavior Lord Amateru concluded that the hatare do not reflect any heavenly purpose but are lesser beings who have discovered the ability to possess ordinary people and control them through their deviant, selfish desires. (In Julius Evola's words they lack "higher consecration.") If the court keeps this in mind, they will be able to find appropriate spiritual means to subdue each group, and the tiny army of 800 soldiers, or *mononobe,* will easily be able to round them up and give them appropriate punishments.

Lord Amateru prepares special weapons for each general to use. The first group of hatare is bewitching the people with visions of fire-breathing serpents. Amateru gives his soldiers magical materials and a chant, causing the witchcraft to disappear. The rebels, realizing defeat, scatter, and the forces of the sovereign simply run after them and subdue them until their leaders are arrested, after which they are sent home.

The second group of hatare is thrown scorpion fish to eat. The rebels, overjoyed, ask their leader how the rival lord, who had been made out to be so evil, could have known of their favorite food. In the ensuing confusion Amateru's general captures the rebel leader and sends the satisfied foot soldiers back where they came.

The third group of hatare is conquered by similar means, using fried treats to distract them from the fight. Upon capturing them Amateru's forces discover that they are not human but are actually the degenerate descendants of an unholy union between a human and a monkey. Lord Amateru kills the lot of them out of mercy, telling them that with their change in heart they will be able to be reborn as humans.

The fourth group of hatare, possessed by foxes and badgers, are distracted with fried rats, which are a fox's favorite food, symbolized by the *aburage* still offered at fox shrines in Japan today (fried curd, not rats, thankfully). When the captured prisoners realize that Amateru is a merciful lord, they join his side and help him round up the rest of the 330,000 rebels. Only the three leaders of this group are punished.

The sixth group of hatare are distracted with oranges in a similar way, and the fifth group are led by disguised monkeys, serpents, badgers, and *nue.** For some reason the fifth group is treated again in the seventeenth aya where it is written that their leader, Hanatoruna, comes to Lord Amateru asking how it is that he is able to promote such a healthy life among his subjects. I will render Amateru's lengthy response in prose:

---

*A legendary creature with the head of a monkey, body of a raccoon, legs of a tiger, and a snake for a tail, able to fly after transforming into a black cloud.

First, the human body is a *hinagata,* meaning a miniature version, of the universe. Our left eye is the Sun, our right eye the Moon, and our nose is a star. The middle of our body is the world: the heart is the sovereign, the liver is the ministers, and the spleen is the common people. The lungs are the workmen, and the kidneys are the merchants. The heart is like a mirror: it shows your true intentions to heaven and Earth, and soon enough men will know of it. This is why one of the Three Treasures of the Emperor is a mirror, the *Yata-no-Kagami.*

The woshite symbol for wo ✪ is two interlocked squares with a point in the middle. If we draw lines from the center to both the outer and inner connections, ✪ is made into sixteen different sections and takes on a resemblance to the chrystanthemum, the imperial symbol, which is only sensible since the ancient word "to rule" is *wo-sameru.* The word for chrysanthemum [in ultra-ancient Japanese] is *koko,* meaning that the heart and mind, *koko-ro,* are one with the mind of the Emperor. The minds of the hatare have therefore become disturbed, and they have lost their reliance on the Emperor.[24]

This explanation of the chrystanthemum conveys important symbolism that can be found in other esoteric texts, but the lesser being Hanatoruna scoffs at this knowledge and departs. Amateru easily defeats him by undoing the curse he has placed on the people, and arrests him as the freed soldiers praise Amateru's ability and conscience. In this way the full force of 709,000 hatare is either persuaded to go home or returned to human form.

Initiation

After many years in his palace Amateru received a messenger bearing news of his teacher Toyoke dying in the country of Miyatsu. Toyoke had already entered his own grave mound and was prepared to die there, so Amateru had to walk into a crypt to bid a tearful good-bye. When he did so, though, Toyoke surprised him with one last message:

"mukashi michinoku

Tsukusaneha

koko ni matsu" to te,

satsukemashi.

"Morokantachi mo

Shika to kike!

Kimi ha ikuyo no

Miwoya nari"

Kore Tokotachi no

Kotonori

"Those years ago, we did not teach Your Majesty
of the Depth of the Way. Now, we complete it," so he said,
and granted it. Then, "Min'sters, too,
now listen up! The Emperor is Parent to
the Countless Ages." Such was Tokotachi's
last message.

The amakami had already learned most of the Ame-naru-Michi,
but the deepest secrets of the Way were not for public consumption, nor
even for the amakami's ministers to hear (the second message seems to
be for a wider audience). Instead they were held back until the very end
of Toyoke's life when Amateru would have the wisdom to keep them,
and on his deathbed Toyoke initiated Amateru into the Way of Heaven.
Such a secret initiation cannot be found anywhere in the official histories or in the other parahistories that I know of. But it is precisely
this initiation that formed the cornerstone of René Guénon's concept
of Tradition.

Much later, in the twenty-third aya, the initiatory "Depth of the
Way" (*michinoku*) is described as being recorded in a secret text called

the Text of Heavenly Being, *Ame-naru-Fumi* ☉ 平 ⊕ 众 ⚠ 帋. The Text is one of the Three Treasures of the Emperor along with the Yata-no-Kagami mirror and Kusanagi-no-Tsuragi sword. Even today, the Emperor of Japan keeps these Three Treasures secret and no one has ever seen them. In the official histories the third treasure is said not to be a document but a *magatama,* a comma-shaped stone of power. But in the *Hotsuma Tsutaye* the use of a text for learning the Way of Heaven is affirmed: in the twenty-seventh aya the spirit of Lord Amateru says that he learned it from a Fragrant Text, *Kagu-no-Fumi* ① 厶 田 ⚠ 帋.

Some years later, after he finished mourning his teacher in Hitakami, Amateru returned to his palace south of Mount Fuji but immediately declared that the palace needed to be moved, and after consulting with augurs and ministers declared that he would move to a place called Isawa—that is to say, Izawa-no-miya! The very same shrine where the *Kujiki*-72 was found becomes the first palace of the initiated Amateru in the *Hotsuma Tsutaye*. According to Rei Torii the *Hotsuma Tsutaye* actually goes beyond the *Kujiki*-72, which merely makes a claim about age, in marking Izawa-no-miya as the place where Amateru gave forth his most important teachings.[25]

Ise-no-Michi

Once at Isawa Lord Amateru propounds the system of living that will inform everything at Ise. In his Way of Ise, *Ise-no-Michi,* a strict set of parallels is set up between the male and female aspects of being. The opposition began with the beginning of the world, when a natural division occured that made the male part rise up and become the heavens and the female part lower and become the Earth. The male and female parts of being are, respectively, Sun and Moon, the tree and its fruit, East and West, positive and negative, active and passive, light and heavy, the First and the Second, beginning and end, *a* and *wa,* red and white, Fire and Water, Wind and Stone, left and right, and heart and veins.

This appears to resemble yin-yang cosmology very closely, except that left and right have been reversed and Japanese elements are used in place of the Chinese ones.[26] There is also a slight resemblance to the

Tachibana-ryu line of secretive, esoteric Buddhism.[27] As in yin-yang cosmology each implies the other, and each cannot exist without the other. The heart cannot live without veins, and without a Second there would be no meaning of First.

Amateru also provides a gloss to the story of his parents Izanami and Izanagi going around the pillar—even if each said their part of the Song of A and Wa correctly, it was still necessary for Izanagi to speak first because the left-facing *a* ② must come at the beginning and the right-facing *wa* ② must come at the end.[28]

The Way of Ise, as Amateru taught it, was an esoteric path to ensure an alchemical marriage, but it did not make sense to everyone. After his death there were many nobles who did not understand it, and in the thirteenth aya his envoy, Kasuga, holds a conference at which he explains it again. Amateru's heir to the throne, Ohonamuchi, does not enjoy being told that he must abstain from wealth seeking and personal desires.

> Said Kasuga, "Suzu is a tree that grows half an inch every year, and withers away when 60,000 years have passed. Then the suzu grows dark (kura), and withers like the family line of a person who only desires wealth. But if a person puts aside personal desires and lives a pure and honest life, the suzu will be bright (ka ①) and the family line will continue in glory."
>
> Now Ohonamuchi, the Lord of Karu, came forward and asked abruptly, "Do you mean to rebuke me for my wealth? I receive nothing but admiration for it!"
>
> Kasuga replied calmly but firmly, "Your thinking is mistaken. While you are alive, you may well be called 'the lord of riches.' But at the end, you will always suffer torment after death."

The Way of Ise always required proper education, and with the end of the Hotsuma civilization it vanished from mainstream society. According to Mitsuru Ikeda, "as the woshite era was coming to an end, people no longer understood the need for such a strict system."[29]

A Calendar to Unite Sun and Moon

In both China and Japan the cycles of the moon and sun were united in a lunisolar calendar based on the Metonic cycle, and according to the *Hotsuma Tsutaye* this was Amateru's invention. Lord Amateru was well aware of the need to balance the solar and lunar principles by replacing the lunar calendar with a lunisolar one. He entrusted the job to his minister Omohikane who made careful observations of the position of the moon and stars. The resulting calendar had twelve months and one intercalary month.

To parallel the new invention Amateru found thirteen consorts, one for every month, and assigned them to imperial houses north, south, east, and west of him, the four compass points representing the four seasons. One of these consorts, Mukatsuhime, attracted Amateru's attention and he made her his wife. The thirteenth consort, whose name Urifu is the origin of the modern word *urū* for "intercalary month," took Mukatsuhime's place in the southern palace. By using his palace to educate the people about the months of the year, Amaterasu did much more than reflect Japanese culture's love of the seasons—he demonstrated understanding not only a cyclical concept of time but also a mapping of the four seasons to the four cardinal points. (Centuries later the *Nihon Shoki* would confuse Amateru himself with his wife Mukatsuhime.)[30]

AMATERASU'S ALCHEMICAL DIET

The last of Lord Amateru's main teachings, in the fifteenth aya, explains how the way the Five Elements balance themselves in our body mandates a pescatarian diet. The amakami explains to a large audience of both nobles and commoners that eating proper food is the way to cleanse one's internal organs, thereby returning body and soul to their original state of perfection. The worst possible food to eat, he said, is that of beasts and birds—doing so pollutes our bodies with their dead spirits and causes us to become weak and sickly. In contrast, vegetables are the best possible to food to eat, since the energy in them comes straight from the

Sun. "If you eat green vegetables," he says, "your muddied blood grown weak with disease will become clear and radiant like the sun."

Amateru's discourse on food is mixed up with an unusual alchemical discourse as he tries to explain the balances of the elements in the various foods and how eating meat will cause imbalance. This portion of his lecture is unlike anything else in premodern Japanese literature:

Listen carefully, all of you.

In the far and distant past, when heaven, earth and man were not yet separate, all was confusion and chaos. Then Amemiwoya (the "Great Parent of the Heavens") blew the first breath into this chaos. Thereupon the heavens quietly started to divide into a female yin part and a male yang part. The light male part rose up into the sky, while the heavy female part sank down to form the earth.

Space from the male part gave birth to Wind, then Wind changed further and separated into Fire. These three original elements of the male, having taken physical shape, rose into the heavens . . . The earth, meanwhile, divided into the two elements of Stone and Water. Stone turned into mountains and countryside, while Water was transformed into lakes and seas. Stone then became mixed with Space in the soil, and the clean and beautiful parts became crystallized as jewels. The pure Stone of the mountains became well penetrated with Space, forming metal ores, while impure Stone turned into mud.

Of these metal ores, those containing more Space were crystallized into tin and lead, those with Stone became gold, and those with Water became silver. Mud turned into copper and iron. The colours of these are yellow like hazel, white like the paulownia blossom, brown like cypress wood, and black like the chestnut.

You must dig up all these ores from the mountains, build tatara furnaces, circulate air through bellows, and refine the ores into metals.

The last commandment comes as somewhat of a surprise. Why does

Amateru ask his people to dig up ore in the mountains? Is he perhaps referring to a process more subtle than the transformation of earth into metal? At least the technology being used is real, and ancient: the tatara method of smelting has existed in Japan since the dawn of history, and its origin is not well understood. In any case, the sermon continues with an explanation of the composition of various foods.

> Flowers and fruits grow according to heavenly providence. Plants and fish made from three elements can be eaten, but not minerals and animals made from two or four. Jewels commonly appear as the crystallization of two elements. Other ores can be refined to produce useful metals.
>
> Insects made from three elements, which feed on water-containing plants, do not normally make any sound. But Wind turns them into beautifully singing creatures. This is the same for insects that fly through the air and those that dwell on the ground.
>
> Birds are made from four elements: Space, Wind, Fire and Water. . . . Wild animals are made from the four elements of Stone, Water, Fire and Wind. . . .
>
> Salt created from the tides of the sea, itself formed through the spirit of the moon, purifies what it touches. We eat salt every day, scatter salt to expel evil spirits, and pile up salt to protect our doorways, because the defilement of our bodies is removed by the mystical power of the moon.
>
> Shellfish are made from the three elements of Water, Stone and Fire, while fish that swim are made from Water, Space and Fire. Fish with scales, in particular, are good to eat and purify our bodies. But fish without scales are made with too much Fire. They should not be eaten because their odor is offensive.

We soon learn that because land animals are missing the element of Space "they have no spirit of the sun or moon. For this reason, if we fall into the realm of the beasts we will be unable to return again in human form." Water fowl can be occasionally eaten if care is taken to make sure their Fire does not overpower the spirit, but land animals are like poison and anyone who eats one should eat nothing but leaves for three days to purify their bodies. It is interesting to note that even though vegetarianism is very rare in Japan the *Hitsuki Shinji* has a similar teaching.

Lord Amateru has an additional, shocking instruction for those who want to become a kami like him. In the age of the kami the "thousand-year plants," or *chiyomi-kusa,* grew at the summit of Mount Fuji. Amateru says that eating the roots of these plants has made him virtually immortal, and that he expects to live for 1.24 million years! However, this plant was so bitter that ordinary human beings considered it inedible. Because its taste was such a trial and because it grew only at the summit of Japan's highest mountain, only true heaven-lords, amakami like Lord Amateru, could eat of it and gain immortality. Unfortunately for would-be seekers, though, woshite researchers generally think that this plant has gone extinct in these latter days.[31]

The chiyomi-kusa does not appear in any other premodern Japanese text, but if Julius Evola had learned of it we might have had the pleasure of seeing his countenance besmirched by a grin. Evola was interested in the symbol of the plant of longevity found in ancient traditions (such as Greek ambrosia, Vedic soma, and Iranian haoma, which grow on high mountains) and felt it was a traditional symbol of inaccessible knowledge of immortality.[32] Chiyomi-kusa not only fits this pattern, it fits it better than any of the Indo-European examples, for it is found at the summit and is inedible to ordinary people.

Finally we learn that the early kami Toyokunnu established a settlement in China, but his descendants in this different climate forgot about the chiyomi-kusa and the correct diet and soon began eating meat and various other forbidden things, shortening their lives to a mere 100 or 200 years. One of Toyokunnu's descendants, Xi Wangmu (a real and archaic divinity who is known to have had offerings made to her over 3,500 years ago), came to Japan, lamenting the situation in China, and was taught the Way.

The *Hotsuma Tsutaye* is actually not the only text giving Japan a more ancient history than China. When the *Nihon Shoki* was privileged as the official Japanese history around 800 CE, the authorities burned two competing histories that claimed that Japan was the origin of several Korean and Chinese dynasties. No copies of these alternative histories survive,[33] but perhaps they may have had some relation to the *Hotsuma Tsutaye*.

This text found in that used bookstore in 1966 is an apparently ancient epic poem the length of the *Aeneid*. It affirms the existence and meaning of thousands of Japanese shrines that are mysterious without it and demonstrates the truth of many traditional beliefs. Despite this, it has never been given so much as a glance by modern Japanese scholars. A serious investigation is warranted.

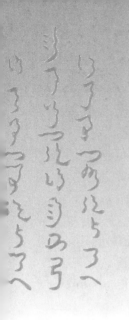

4
Japanese Atlantis, Christ, and Pyramids

The Takenouchi Documents

"In the world of Tradition," writes Julius Evola, "the most important foundation of authority and of the right of kings and chiefs, and the reason why they were obeyed, feared, and venerated, was essentially their transcendent and nonhuman quality."[1] What if a prestigious noble family possessed secret records of this world of Tradition millions of years ago? Would you want to read them? Most people would certainly call any such documents unbelievable, an obvious fraud. But some fraction of the population, perhaps including some readers of this book, will surely be intrigued by the possibility of a direct transmission from the Traditional realm, and for some among them the discovery of the Takenouchi Documents will confirm the truth that they have known all their lives.

As we will see the Takenouchi Documents must be interpreted as more of a revelation than a strict historical document. We must possess an imagination that allows us to travel into their deep past and see it for ourselves, then come back to the present realizing the connections to the world around us. By doing so we embed the Japanese tradition into the traditions of the world, giving the *sophia perennis,* the universal wisdom shared in fragments by all peoples, a much more complex historical form and narrative.

The Documents captured the hearts of many spiritualists in the imperial period, the greatest such figure being the parahistorian, adventurer, and eccentric Katsutoki Sakai (1874–1940). Notable postwar researchers include such personalities as New Age essayist Wado Kōsaka (1947–2002), and Mikoto M. Nakazono (1918–1994), disciple of aikido founder Morihei Ueshiba.

It must be emphasized, though, that the Documents were never endorsed by anyone of authority in Japan, and were both confiscated by the government for over a decade and ridiculed by academics forever after. I will return to the subject of politics later, but suffice to say these independently produced documents are outside the mainstream view of history. They are, like the other texts in this book, parahistorical.

JAPAN GRAPPLES WITH THE UNIVERSALIST THREAT

When the Takenouchi Documents are revealed, early modern Japan is no longer sealed off from the West, as with the previous two parahistories, but is now a reborn nation thrust onto the world stage. The people of Japan have discovered the existence not just of neighboring empires, but also of rival traditions that speak of one God for all the nations, a god who has had only a few prophets and whose message applies equally to every human being on Earth. The Japanese can compete with the technological and material success of Western colonialism by imitating its methods, but they are unable to imitate the teachings of the West.

What Japan is being asked to do around the turn of the nineteenth century is somewhat paradoxical. To successfully imitate the modern forms of statehood demanded by Westerners, it is necessary to inculcate obedience to the state. Many European nations at this time had a state church and a monarch who drew his authority from divine right. But from the beginning of Japan's relations with the modern West, diplomacy and international treaties, especially with America, demanded that Japan preserve a "separation of church and state" and allow Christians to proselytize freely. Japan's solution was to declare a secular, semi-Confucian state ruled by a secular emperor, but an emperor whose lineage is unbroken as described in the *Kojiki* and *Nihon Shoki*, and whose authority is absolute. This political system was not intended to direct people's daily lives and behavior.[2]

The *Kojiki* and *Nihon Shoki*, like the Hebrew Bible, say little about other nations of the world. They are the chronicles of the Japanese emperors. But in the 1920s, even as the chronicles are taught in the textbooks of the Japanese Empire, their local history of a single island is being attacked by universalist Christian missionaries and "religious scholars," the most notorious of which persuades the West that Japan's political system is an "old communal form" of an imagined universal "religion," which is allegedly *not* meant to be political and is meant to direct people's daily lives, except that it has failed to "progress" beyond a "primitive way of life."[3] These learned scholars do not and cannot explain how they know that some stories about the past are "religions," which are meant to "progress" from communal to universal, but for the most part, the Japanese do not take up this line of questioning—the questions are complicated, and the language barrier is high.

What spiritual responses appear to this bullying? Some Japanese people and Westerners assert Japan has some ancient relationship with the Hebrew nation, which is allowed to teach its children their ancestral heritage without the demand for development. The theory of Jewish ancestry, and its proponents, have been well documented in other books.* Other Japanese discover new religions, such as Konkokyo and Tenrikyo, which aim to create a monotheism based in Japanese forms. Still others surrender their traditions entirely and convert to

---

*Nicholas McLeod's *Epitome of the Ancient History of Japan* (Nagasaki: Rising Sun Office, 1878) is a good summary of evidence for Jewish origins found by that author, some of which is still mentioned by proponents today. The 130 years of research and discoveries since then are well summarized in the first part of Samuel Lee's *Rediscovering Japan, Reintroducing Christendom: Two Thousand Years of Christian History in Japan* (Hamilton, 2010).

Christianity. The great majority, though, carry on with the vague premise that they live in a nation whose origins can be found somewhere in the depths of the *Kojiki* and *Nihon Shoki*. The challenge that this worldview faces from Christianity, in the guise of "world opinion," is severe.

The Western world of the imperial period is the progeny of Christendom, and despite diplomatic acceptance of Japan there is still a guarded suspicion toward the nation's perceived lack of "spiritual development" toward wholesome universalism. The deep hypocrisy of the West on these subjects is betrayed at the Paris Peace Conference of 1919 when the Japanese delegation fights long and hard for the nations of the world to agree to a policy of racial equality, but is ultimately defeated by a coalition of European and American interests. Clearly, Japan *does* have something to offer the world, but the fundamental principles the Japanese base their society on are hard to articulate.

The Takenouchi Documents provide such a universal principle. They proclaim that the legends of the *Kojiki* and *Nihon Shoki* are, despite their radically different appearance, part of a grand ultra-ancient Tradition that is *one and the same* with the teachings of Christianity, Islam, and Buddhism, and the Japanese should therefore follow their spiritual convictions to create a better world. In trying to tap into this Tradition, the Documents hit on a message that was relevant not only to Japan but also to Europe.

These Documents, which first appeared in 1928, describe an ultra-ancient planet united under a line of World-Emperors. Only a few years earlier a Polish professor named Ferdinand Ossendowski had published a book called *Beasts, Men, and Gods* in which he described his dangerous escape from the Soviet Union, through Siberia, and into the Buddhist kingdom of Mongolia and the legends he heard there of the King of the World. Ossendowski's book caused such an international stir that the French metaphysician René Guénon used it as the basis for his most controversial work, *The King of the World*. Guénon argued that Ossendowski's book joined countless religious texts and ancient legends attesting to an original sacred center ruled by a King of the

World. But neither Guénon nor other commentators were aware that another text on the other side of the world had positively identified this sacred land and its king.

CREATION OF A PLANETARY EMPIRE

Innumerable billions of years ago, the Takenouchi Documents tell us, the world was a sea of mud. After twenty-two billion years of formation, out of All emerged the first God and Goddess, and the heavens and the Earth were separated and became a firmament. The Earth hardened and became a sphere. The God and Goddess gave birth to another couple, representing the Sun and Moon respectively, and in this way the Earth took form for six generations.

DYNASTIES OF THE WORLD-EMPERORS[4]

DYNASTY	LENGTH	DESCRIPTION OF LEADERSHIP
Genesis	Unknown	Seven timeless generations of Creator Gods. In Japanese, *Amatsu Kami*
High Ancient	300 billion years	World-Emperor travels around the world regularly ensuring proper government and teaching universal laws. In Japanese, *Jōko or Kamiyo*
Fukiaezu	3 million years	World-Emperor loses material prosperity but continues to send teachers around the world. Named after Emperor Jimmu's father Ugayafukiaezu
Kamu Yamato	Since 660 BCE	The present, degenerate age. Teachers and prophets come to Japan. Named after the Yamato tribe

The fifth generation God and Goddess gave birth to the Creator of the Nations and his wife who descended to Mt. Kurai in Japan and took on "shining bodies." In the seventh generation various beings developed technologies for life on Earth such as transportation and writing. The first calendar was made, consisting of twelve thirty-day months: Mutsuhi, Kesari, Iyayo, Ubeko, Sanae, Minatsu, Fukumi, Hayare, Nayona, Kaname, Shiburu, and Shihatsu, which were followed by intercalary days. Each month consisted of three ten-day weeks called Tatsu, Mado, and Komori.

The seventh generation Sun God declared the beginning of the lineage of World-Emperors, called *Sumera-Mikoto* ΛᎢᑎᕼ ᎫᖾᎤᏦ ᎢᏞᏟᏞ in ultra-ancient Japanese. He also set out the islands of Japan as distinct from the rest of the planet, naming Japan "the Land of Hidama" or the Sun-Sphere. Today Japan remains the only nation that fights under the flag of the rising sun, but in ancient times the scribes still spoke of the Egyptian king reigning from "the seat of Horus," the Persian ruler "who rises in the company of the sun," and the Roman *sol invictus.* In fact, so many ancient cultures preserved the solar symbol that James Churchward claimed it was evidence of a lost sun empire called Mu, and Julius Evola was convinced that it was a remnant of an era of Tradition that no longer survives in writing.[5]

The name Sumera-Mikoto is broken down by Wado Kōsaka into many component symbols, including the center, the unification, the Sun, the seed, the masculine principle of Yang, and "human characteristics."[6] The Takenouchi Documents refer to the Sumera-Mikoto as the "Son of the Sun" since he was descended from the Sun God. According to Guénon this is a title of the *Vaivasvata Manu,* the Indian name for the King of the World.[7]

The Sun God's heir began the High Ancient dynasty and after eight billion years dispatched his sons and daughters around the planet to found their own nations. He divided the world into sixteen sections, one for each new *mittoson,* a sort of king or vassal. These kings became the *Five-Colored Peoples*—white, blue, red, yellow, and black—and were scattered across the continents in no particular pattern. Here, an excerpt from Plato's description of Atlantis may prove intriguing: "My grandfather had the original writing, which is still in my possession, and was carefully studied by me when I was a child . . . I have before remarked in speaking of the allotments of the gods, that they distributed the whole Earth into portions differing in extent, and made for themselves temples and instituted sacrifices."[8]

Some of these founding kings are named in the following excerpt:

> On the 10th of Sanae, in the 1,030,000,000th year of the reign of the Sumera-Mikoto, the Sumera-Mikoto descended on Mt. Hirefure in Yomoitsu [Europe]. The King of the red-colored race Adameve, the King of the white-colored race Koratomamusu, and the King of the blue-colored race Kiambocha paid a visit to the Sumera-Mikoto, and were then appointed as the Mittoson over the places where they resided.[9]

We appear to be in the era of Eden, but in this version "Adameve" is a single man and the king of the "red-colored race," while at almost the same time on the other side of the world, Guénon was writing that "the literal meaning of the name Adam is 'red' and [we] can see in it one indication of the link of the Hebraic tradition to the Atlantean tradition, which was that of the *red race*" [emphasis added].[10] Why does Guénon have a parallel with this text that he never saw, in naming Adam as the leader of a long-forgotten red race?

After the establishment of the sixteen nations the World-Emperor's role became to tour the world to ensure that the peace and rule of the Sun were being kept among the Five-Colored Peoples. In high ancient times the World-Emperor was able to travel all over the world on a flying ship called *Ame-no-Ukifune* ㅏ口ㅐㄴㅗ丁ㅣㅎ丁ㄴ, literally, the "floating ship of heaven." Using this ship he could visit all the mittoson in a matter of years rather than decades. Actually, the Ame-no-Ukifune was long known to Japanese historians before the Takenouchi Documents appeared. The *Nihon Shoki* and the *Kujiki*-10 both describe a flying ship called Ame-no-Iwafune on which the ancestor of the Mononobe clan named Nigihayahi descended to Earth.[11] In the Takenouchi Documents this ship was used by the gods to descend to Earth, but thereafter became the exclusive property of the World-Emperor who lent it out only on rare occasions.

The Ame-no-Ukifune were said to require good takeoff and landing spots. Such ancient airports would be named with the Japanese word *hane* meaning "wing." Even today places named Hane can be found all over the world, most notably Haneda Airport in Tokyo. One Takenouchi researcher has found nine such Hane airports lying on a vertical ley line resembling an ancient Prime Meridian running through the middle of Japan. At the northern end of this ley line (located at 137° 11′ east) is a pyramid-shaped mountain called Tongari-yama that is a modern UFO hot spot.[12]

When he arrived in a place the World-Emperor would be met with awe. Writes Wado Kōsaka: "It is easy to imagine the extreme anxiety of the Mittoson who had to receive the Sumera-Mikoto without prior notice. For the five-colored peoples who were suffering from misgovernment, the world visits by the Sumera-Mikoto were opportunities for relief, and thus the Sumera-Mikoto was always welcomed with the highest honor and respect in very land."[13] The World-Emperor never had to use force but could replace a bad king simply through proclamation, echoing Evola's assertion that Traditional rule "did not need physical strength to assert itself, and when it did, it was only sporadically. It imposed itself mainly and irresistibly through the spirit."[14] All people were taught about the origin and the authority of the Sumera-Mikoto so his judgment could resolve any dispute and ensure complete peace.

Besides being the ultimate source of law, the World-Emperor developed technologies for the sake of the people. Each World-Emperor had his own form of writing; the first generation used pictograms, but by the fourth generation the kamiyo moji had become more abstract, being the basis of Ahiru script 아δΙ JTLＬδΤΟΙ, and the fifth generation used Ahiru brush script. Later generations developed still more forms of writing, until eventually they resembled modern katakana.

While the Japanese of this era were *Hibito,* People of the Sun, and were given special duties to maintain the imperial teachings, the World-Emperors themselves only lived in Japan and were not themselves Japanese. Rather, they were above all colors and married women of pure heart, called *Kisakinomiya,* from all over the world. When no male heirs were produced there would be a World-Empress who would marry a man of pure heart called *Yosachio*. The practice of selecting a spouse from among the Five-Colored Peoples ended in the Fukiaezu dynasty, which seems associated with the decline of the World-Emperor's power.[15] From that point on the World-Emperor was forced more and more to limit his activities to Japan, and only the Hibito were dispatched around the world to continue education programs.

The Great Concealment

In *The King of the World* Guénon finds sufficient witnesses in "the concordant testimonies of all traditions" to conclude that "there is a 'Holy Land' par excellence, that it is the prototype for all other 'Holy Lands,' and that it is the spiritual center to which all others are subordinate. The 'Holy Land' is also the 'Land of the Saints,' the 'Land of the Blessed,' the 'Land of the Living,' and the 'Land of Immortality.'"[16] We have found that Japan can be described in all of these terms in the Takenouchi Documents. Furthermore, the World-Emperor is very much a Guénonian King of the World.

Guénon proceeds to say that this land was available to us only in past ages, hundreds of thousands of years ago, and that it is now "invisible and inaccessible." Japan is very much visible and accessible today—does that count against the symbolic authority of the Takenouchi Documents? In fact, it counts for them, for just as the Holy Land was closed at the beginning of the Kali Yuga, the spiritual center of Japan was sealed at the beginning of the present age and will not be reopened until our age of material power ends.

As the world took form it was also rocked by cataclysms, earthquakes, and floods, attested in texts all over the world. In the Takenouchi Documents these are described as *Tenpenchii* and there are not one but dozens of them over the course of history, caused by an imbalance in the order of heaven. Over the course of history the Tenpenchii grew steadily more severe. In fact two whole continents called *Miyoi* and *Tamiara* in the Pacific Ocean sank (parallels to Mu, Atlantis, and Lemuria are clear, but the Documents say little about these continents other than that they existed and later sank). The World-Emperor was forced to scale back his activities, and eventually ended them. Two different researchers of the Documents have offered different theories as to how this happened.

Wado Kōsaka calls the Tenpenchii a result of disobedience: "While people were enjoying highly civilized society guided by the Sumera-Mikoto, arrogance took root in the heart of humanity. The kings of the five colored peoples gained power over the Sumera-Mikoto, lost respect toward the Sumera-Mikoto and began to ignore and despise him."[17] As long as the people had faith in the World-Emperor, though, he could simply use his authority to replace any bad governor, so surely the great age of world-empire could not have been put to an end by rebellions alone.

Mikoto Nakazono offers a more subtle explanation: Education, not only in obedience to the World-Emperor but also in basic principles of mindfulness and law, was becoming steadily more difficult as the world became more separated. Despite thousands of years of efforts by the World-Emperors and their delegates to raise the level of the Five-Colored Peoples to enlightenment, writes Nakazono, the incarnated humans could not maintain a high level of consciousness:

> Ordinary people simply could not see the point. Why spend so much time and energy listening to teachers, why go through such discipline, why go hungry, sleep, meditate . . .
>
> In the end, the younger leaders came before their elders saying, "We have worked for forty thousand years to make a perfect society, and we have not succeeded because the people cannot understand us . . . How much longer must we go on? In the end, this will make a greater sacrifice than the development of a material situation ever could. Please, give us the permission to guide society in this direction. If we cannot bring them to understand the activity of their senses, they must explore it for themselves. If we guide them straight to the mark, it can be done so much more quickly."

The discussion went on for a long time. Finally, the elder god-men agreed. They gave their consent, asking only that the work be begun as far away from Hinomoto Kuni as possible.[18]

Takenouchi researchers generally believe that the work indeed began on the other side of the world, and that the first group to be seg-regated from the universal rule of the Sumera-Mikoto was the ancient Middle Eastern civilization of the Fertile Crescent, who out of love for their former leader named themselves the Sumerians.[19]

Nakazono interprets the Documents as saying that over many decades the teachings were slowly wound up and then disguised as myth, religion, and spiritual messages "in competition" with matter in order to allow a material society to develop and flourish. But the perennial tradition, which he calls the Kototama Principle, remains hidden underneath these various disguises to be unveiled after material civilization reaches its natural conclusion. This is all in accordance with Guénon, who wrote "it is more true to say that the tradition is hidden rather than lost, or at least that it can be lost only to certain secondary spiritual centers that have ceased to remain a direct contact with the supreme center."[20]

There are many disguised references to the original principles in today's spiritual messages. The dispute between Susanowo and Amaterasu in the *Kojiki*, Nakazono says, is a disguised account of the battle between earthly desires, *Kanagi,* and the higher dimensions of Kototama or *Futonorito.* Furthermore, "from the oldest religions to Islam, the most recent, all dogmas symbolize the Kototama Principle."[21] As we will learn next, the Takenouchi family preserved the initiation into the Principle at their Grand Shrine to the Imperial Ancestors, *Kōso Kōtai Jingū,* located in modern Toyama City, and all the spiritual teach-ers of the world learned the Principle from there.

Wado Kōsaka made the same discovery in the course of his research: the continuous Tenpenchii century after century had made world unity impossible, and Japanese culture had been decimated. Therefore, the program of "heart and spirit" ended, and the Five-Colored Peoples were asked to pursue logic and physical sciences to their fullest extents. Once this development completes, Kōsaka says, the next step will be to "combine the values of ultra-ancient civilization and the values of modern civilization."[22]

By the time the Yamato dynasty was founded Japan no longer possessed the technology and abilities it once had. Perhaps these, too, were purposefully demolished in the great concealment. In fact ordinary people no longer even knew how to write the kamiyo moji, and basic skills had to be imported from China and Korea. But the Takenouchi family for their part still possessed the ancient secrets of writing and technology, and the Emperor still reigned. Notably, the real historical figure Takenouchi no Sukune, who is claimed by the *Kojiki* to have lived for over 300 years, apparently commissioned the Takenouchi Documents in the first century CE and was still able to use the Ame-no-Ukifune then. But for the sake of world salvation, the heavenly way required new, non-Japanese sages.

Jesus's Ninja Training and Moses's UFO Journey

At this point the symbolic world of the Takenouchi Documents becomes completely outrageous. But perhaps an outraged reaction is evidence that people are uncomfortable with the truth. So I will press on with my narrative, keeping in mind that Guénon, when trying to understand the difficult and hidden teachings of the King of the World, made use of accounts that he knew were faulty, incomplete, or even a "caricature" of the truth since the existence of such accounts symbolizes deeper forces at work.[23]

The Takenouchi family preserved the Documents in urns lying in secret locations beneath the ground of Kōso Kōtai Jingū, awaiting the day when the world would be able to understand the history they revealed, making themselves available only to select foreign teachers— none of their students were Japanese, although the reason for this is not given. Unfortunately the original manuscripts of these teachers' accomplishments did not survive World War II, but fragments are preserved in the journals of General Yutarō Yano (1881–1938) and a Christian named Kiku Yamane (1893–1965), whose first book *A Light from the East* appeared in 1938.*

The most notable such teacher, both for us and for Takenouchi researchers, was Jesus. Occultists may be familiar with Nicholas Notovich's claim that Jesus made a pilgrimage to India in his teens to study Buddhist philosophy, returning to Israel at the age of thirty to teach what he had learned. For the Takenouchi proponents, who clearly regard Japan as a sort of Shambhala whose wisdom is open only to a select few, Jesus's journey took him past the classical centers of India to the true center in Japan. After stopping in India, Jesus, a fully human son of Mary and Joseph whose real name was apparently Jesuchri Christmas, continued his journey to Kōso Kōtai Jingū, where the head priest, seeing his innate abilities, subjected him to what Wado Kōsaka calls "ninja training."[24]

According to Yamane Kiku, Jesus "acquired the ability to perform approximately twenty divine arts out of fifty or so. Curing diseases is the preliminary stage of the divine art. The divine techniques include the skill to disappear, jumping up or down from a tall tree which is so tall that one cannot see the top, walking on the surface of the water with a bamboo rod that is thrown onto the sea or the river, walking in the air, purifying a room or the soil." Jesus returned to Israel to demonstrate the great spiritual messages and ninja abilities of the divine principle, but he became a wanted man. His brother, Isukiri, met with the disciples and agreed to die in his place; it is this brother, not Jesus, who Judas handed over to the Romans.[25]

Jesus himself returned to Japan to continue his study with fourteen new disciples from around the world, including men of Japanese, Ainu, Italian, German, Native American, Australian, Jewish, Roman, and African ancestry. He traveled around the world spreading

---

*The founder of an unrelated Japanese religious group, the Church of World Messianity, had an interesting saying, *Tōkō-Seiki* 東光西輝, meaning "light from the East shall illuminate the West"—Japanese people think this saying is odd in that the light from the East is not illuminating the East itself, but perhaps there is something to be said for it.

teachings of peace and love, and died on December 25, 82 CE, at the respectable age of 118, after which he was buried in Japan. His tomb there was rediscovered in 1934 and can still be visited today in Herai village in Aomori. A relic he made from the ashes of his parents (fig. 4.1) was once discovered there but was destroyed during the Pacific War.

Mose Romulus, alias Moses, also came to Japan in order to understand the principles of law. As leader of the Jews and rightful king of the Five-Colored Races, he was somewhat busier than Jesus and did not have a lot of free time to walk to Japan, so the Emperor lent him use of the Ame-no-Ukifune, which picked him up on the top of Mt. Sinai. In that era the Ame-no-Ukifune was no longer familiar to the Five-Colored Races, and we can only imagine that a flying ship passing overhead high in the sky would have resembled a UFO to the people down below. The Takenouchi Documents themselves do not say much about Moses, but artifacts discovered by their proponents do, and will be discussed below. The grave of Moses, where his artifacts were discovered, is in Hakui in Ishikawa prefecture, and has been visited by the Israeli Japanologist Ben-Ami Shillony.[26]

Other foreign masters who studied at Kōso Kōtai Jingū include Shakyamuni Buddha, Lao-Tzu, Confucius, Mencius, Xu Fu, and Mohammed. Most of them did not leave relics behind, but the shrine-keeper reported their commitment and the skills they learned.

Time for Reawakening

At one point in the seventh century, it is claimed, Japanese court bureaucrats raided Kōso Kōtai Jingū, attempting to root out the true lineage of the Emperor. The only text that the family surrendered, though, was a geneaology of the Yamato dynasty called *Sumera-Mikoto no Hitsugi,* which is in fact named as one of the source texts for the *Kojiki.* Throughout the classical period and the Middle Ages, Kōso Kōtai Jingū successfully kept up a pretense of being just another little family shrine, and as late as 1912 they were not claiming any link to Takenouchi no Sukune. They even dropped the "no" from their names.

Figure 4.1. A stone carving made by Jesus using the ashes of his parents, Mary and Joseph.

(Another person named Takeuchi claims that this is proof that these people are not the real heirs of Takenouchi no Sukune, and that he possesses the True Takenouchi Documents, which they altered by inserting references to Christ and so forth, but I will not pursue his claims in this book.)[27]

In 1893 the patriarch of the Takeuchi family passed away. In his will he informed his grandson Kiyomaro Takeuchi (1874/5–1965) that the world was rapidly changing and the family's treasures and documents were to be released when the world had become sufficiently peaceful. Kiyomaro put aside the question for a while and moved to a temple called Kurama-dera to undergo ritual training (fig 4.2). This unusual esoteric temple, Buddhist at the time, today worships a being said to have come from Venus 6.5 million years ago, identified by some writers with Theosophy's Ascended Master Sanat Kumara. While at this temple Kiyomaro told a visiting travel writer that his household possessed divine texts and special abilities, but he declined to show them. He later moved from Toyama to Ibaraki, taking the documents with him. Finally, in 1928, Kiyomaro made public the most important texts of the divine age.

By 1929 Kiyomaro had roughly a hundred interested people doing research on the texts,[28] but the Japanese secret police eventually took him to trial and seized the documents and treasures, which were apparently destroyed during firebombing in World War II. After the war the American Occupation banned Kiyomaro from writing or preaching, so he was unable to reconstruct the Documents.[29] Today, only a few photocopies and relics remain, as well as the remainder of the Documents, which are still buried underground until the time is right.

We may wonder what exactly happened between 1893 and 1928 that made the twentieth century the right time to release the texts. The enigmatic figure of Kiyomaro is not very helpful, and even the most rigorous skeptical studies have not been able to learn very much about him, but one of his associates was much more public in his adventures and deserves a close study.

*Figure 4.2. Kiyomaro Takeuchi undergoing ascetic training
at Kurama-dera, while he waited to release the Takenouchi Documents.*

THE HERETICAL DISCOVERIES
OF KATSUTOKI SAKAI

As the Takenouchi Documents were being uncovered Katsutoki Sakai had just returned from world travels where he had discovered the sacred geometry of the Great Pyramids. For some reason Sakai has never had the honor of an English-language biography, even though he is a rather infamous character in the Japanese occult world. Only a brief sketch can be attempted here. A native of Tohoku and a Christian convert, Sakai was raised from poverty with the help of American missionaries and teachers, moved to San Francisco in 1898, and attended the Moody Bible Institute in Chicago from 1899–1902 where he was given the nickname "Vio" for his love of the violin. He worked prolifically while in America: studying full-time, editing a Japanese newspaper, and authoring several English-language articles on music, which are brimming with rhapsody and a pleasure to read:

> The universe seems just a great world of music. Let us go wherever we will, still we hear a harmonic sound which the great American poet, Emerson, called "a sky-born music." . . . Issai Sato, a Japanese scholar, says: "A breath, a tongue, is also music." Music is, indeed, the breath of the universe, consisting of natural order and harmony; in a word, it is the voice of Nature; and it may be the Heavenly voice.[30]

After graduating Sakai taught Christian hymns in Tokyo for a while and published his thoughts on music and the nature of body and soul. The turning point of his life came on the evening of June 7, 1914, when he looked up at the moon and saw it had a faint halo around it. He idly remembered that the halo was an ancient Far Eastern omen for coming war, but just as he was thinking that, he was shocked to see two beams of light deface the moon, forming a right cross (fig. 4.3). As he watched he felt touched by the Divine, and later wrote that "even in my transfixion I could not suppress my ecstasy," and "mine heart felt as if it had seen Heaven, that I had glimpsed a Thought come from

Figure 4.3. Sakai's illustration of his vision of the Sun Cross,
which had mystical significance for him.

Heaven." Sakai realized his vision was incredibly meaningful but in the days afterward he could not make sense of it. What did it mean to have war followed by the Cross? Two weeks later, Archduke Franz Ferdinand was assassinated, sparking World War I.[31]

The Democratic-Humanist Conspiracy

Stationed with the Japanese Army in Harbin, Sakai saw for himself the horror of modern war, and his pacifist Christianity transformed into a complex antimodernism. In his excellent biography *Katsutoki Sakai: "Heretical" Missionary* (2012) Masafumi Kume writes, "Sakai's antimodernism was not merely anachronism, but was rather a sort

Figure 4.4. Katsutoki Sakai.

of idealism that aimed to leverage alternative ways of thinking to reimagine civilization." He began an intent study of the Christian Armageddon, and what sort of society would be established at modernity's end. His vision of the cross in the moon became a symbol that Japan (the moon, or sun?) and Christianity (the cross) shared a joint destiny. Perhaps Japan would have a role to play in a transformative, positive Armageddon.[32]

In 1918 Sakai was sent to Vladivostok to work as a translator for the Japanese arm of a joint West-East alliance against Communism. Oddly enough, Ferdinand Ossendowski, who later gave the Western world its first taste of the King of the World symbology, was working for the Mongolian branch of that same alliance under the monarchist cavalry army of "Bloody Baron" Roman von Ungern-Sternberg, of whom Julius Evola wrote:

> Descended from an old Baltic family, Ungern-Sternberg can be regarded as the last implacable enemy of the Bolshevik Revolution, which he fought with a relentless and inextinguishable hatred. His principal feats of arms proceeded in an atmosphere saturated with magic and the supernatural, in the heart of Asia, under the reign of the Dalai Lama, the "living Buddha."[33]

As shown on the map (fig. 4.5) Ossendowski did intelligence work in the Bloody Baron's capital of Urga while Sakai was working in the Allied protectorate of Vladivostok, but in between the two of

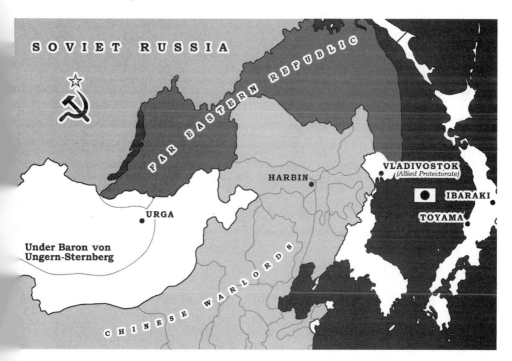

Figure 4.5. The Far East in May 1921. In Urga Ossendowski consulted with the Living Buddha, while Sakai read the Protocols *in Vladivostok.*

them lay a treacherous terrain of Chinese warlords and the short-lived Communist puppet state, the Far Eastern Republic. While both writers spoke English, there is no record that their paths crossed.

Instead Sakai plunged into anti-Semitic texts taken from the White Russians, including the *Protocols of the Elders of Zion,* and he soon became a national expert on the "global Jewish conspiracy." His goal was to uncover how this conspiracy could hasten the end of the world and the coming of the Messiah. This meant, at first, that he fully accepted the concept of a Jewish conspiracy ruining Western nations from within—and supported it as God's work. As he returned home from Siberia, though, he realized that the truth was more complicated.

According to Sakai's theory, secretive groups like the Freemasons had long ago forced the Jews from their country, were behind antistate revolutions in France, America, and Russia, and now were manipulating the Americans and Russians especially to force people into egalitarian democracy and communism, but the Jews were working against them to repel modernity and create a worldwide theocracy. Soon the Jews would come to Japan and unite with their long-lost brethren to restore Jewish-Japanese theocracy to the world. Japanese people needed to be wary, not of the Jews, but of the manipulated Americans.[34]

In 1927 Sakai offered to investigate the Jewish problem for the Japanese Army, and he was dispatched to Palestine with a Judaica scholar named Norihiro Yasue (1886–1950), who we will meet again later. While Yasue met with David Ben-Gurion and other influential Zionists, Sakai visited the Pyramids in Giza and the Mount of Olives in Jerusalem. He purchased olive seeds there that he brought back to Mount Koya and placed on the grave of Mrs. Elizabeth Anna Gordon (1851–1925), a holistic writer who lived in Japan for twenty years writing about links between the Christian and Far Eastern traditions. Her books such as *Symbols of 'The Way'* (1916) remain enlightening today.[35]

The Secret Ten Commandments

Soon after returning to Japan, Sakai became a close associate of Kiyomaro Takeuchi. Reading the Takenouchi Documents, he realized that it was not the Jews who would come to help the Japanese, but the Japanese who were the original Center that produced the Jews. He recognized the truth in the Documents immediately and became deeply engaged in searching for archaeological validation of their claims. Visiting what Takeuchi claimed to be Moses's gravesite in Ishikawa prefecture, Sakai discovered a number of artifacts with strange writing on them, and took them to Takeuchi for confirmation. Takeuchi first denied that he knew of such artifacts, but when pressed he went to the shrine's treasure house and brought back another object with the same script on it. These objects contain the Front and Back 10 Commandments of Moses.

The Front Commandments mostly resemble those of the Hebrew Bible, but the Back Commandments, identified with the original tablet Moses destroyed when he saw the golden calf, are all new. The stone reads "We report the universal laws of Romulus, 60th Generation descendant of Adameve," followed by this list:

1. Thou shalt obey the True God of Heaven *Nihon*
2. Thou shalt obey the True Hitsuki (Sun and Moon) God
3. Thou shalt not disobey the Sun God, for if thou dost thou shalt be smited
4. Thou shalt not disobey the law of the God of Heaven
5. Thou shalt not disobey the True Emperor
6. Thou shalt protect the laws of the Five-Colored Peoples of Ajichi (Heaven-and-Earth)
7. Thou shalt not disobey the law of the True People of Ajichi, the decided law of the ancestral land of Ajichi
8. Thou shalt rescue the red (pure) of heart, and correct the black of heart
9. Thou shalt inform thyself of the stories of other kami
10. Thou shalt worship the Sun God—ABERU, HI, O, ĀMEN![36]

This artifact is signed "The law of all nations. Mount Sinai, Ten Commandments of Moses." Now, there is something very unusual about this text. One would expect it to be some sort of imitation or elaboration of the Front Commandments in the same way that the *Kujiki*-72 provided an elaboration of Prince Shōtoku's Constitutions. But in fact there are no specific laws named here. These "Ten Commandments" do not command any sort of morality, and Evola would recognize this as a memory of Tradition. Quoting the *Tao Te Ching*'s statement "when the Tao was lost, its attributes appeared," Evola wrote that the laws of the traditional era "could not be reduced in any way to the domain of morality in the current sense of the word."[37] The Bible's story is that Moses smashed his first tablet upon seeing the golden calf. Perhaps he realized that the Israelites were not prepared to understand the teaching of the Back Commandments.

With the help of the Takenouchi Documents, Sakai's cosmology was completed. He came to see Japan as holding the unique ability to create true world peace by establishing divine theocracy under a restored World-Emperor. He identified the World-Emperor with the child mentioned in the Book of Revelation "who will rule the nations with an iron scepter," and Japan with the "place prepared by God" where the child will be hidden for 1,260 days (there being 1,260 years between Prince Shōtoku's Constitution and the Meiji Restoration). Now the time had come for the Emperor of Japan to take his place above and beyond nations.[38]

But at the same time Sakai explictly warned that this could not be a justification for war or racial supremacy and wrote in 1930 that "just as the Sun would not allow itself to be monopolized by one nation, the Emperor will not permit domination by one nation or one people. The Emperor, the Son of the Sun, must work for the happiness of all nations as he did in the Kamiyo."[39] Both he and his parahistorian friend General Yutarō Yano joined the Japan Esperanto Society and demonstrated their unique quest for true universalism by writing some of Japan's first Esperanto texts, while at the same time searching for the original, pre-Babel universal language in Japan's ancient relics. Sakai believed that the propagation of English as an international language was a modernist, imperialist initiative, and from 1920 on it appears that he no longer wrote in English, although his ability remained superior.[40]

Pyramids of Antique Japan

On April 23, 1934, Sakai, exhausted after a long mountain hike through pouring rain, looked up at Mount Ashitake towering before him and suddenly had a flash of insight. He turned to his fellow hikers and spoke: "Gentlemen, that mountain is surely a *pyramid.*"[41] Within a year he authored and published a book called *Pyramids of Antique Japan* ᎤᏓᏂᏟᎣᏏᎠᏍᎢᎦᏀᎢᎦᏐᎢᏟᏕᏟᏆ, which proposed that Mount Ashitake and other oddly shaped mountains had been purposefully shaped into pyramids 23,000 years ago. He also discovered stone outcrops that resemble large artificial pillars and various mythical beasts.

Residents of rural areas who learned that mountains in their region were pyramids would naturally become very excited and would come to listen to Sakai's talks in large numbers. Sakai would inevitably tell them that the *Kojiki* and *Nihon Shoki* were not telling the truth about Japan's history. The secret police were not amused by these goings-on. Believing Sakai's pyramid cosmology to be a threat to Japan's educational regime, they seized and destroyed all the copies of *Pyramids of Antique Japan* they could find, and put restrictions on Sakai's movements. This book is now legendary in the Japanese occult world, in part because it is very rare. No libraries in Japan carry the first edition.

Sakai was unfazed by the police attention. A seemingly tireless adventurer, he did not rest on his laurels having found ancient Japanese pyramids and proof that Moses came to Japan, but journeyed on to the outskirts of Tohoku to search for *hihiirokane*, a tough, stainless metal found in the Takenouchi Documents, which he identified with the orichalcum mentioned in Plato's account of Atlantis. He also became a parahistory researcher, announcing in books like *100 Secrets of the Age of the Kami* ᎢᏛᎤᏃᏣᏞᏞᎣᏃᏝᏛᎯᎱ that the Japanese legend of *Momotaro* ("Peach Boy") has its origins in an ultra-ancient prince of the World-Emperor's Court, and identifying the Hifumi Song of the *Kujiki*-72 as being a transmission of an original Japanese set of numerals, which extend to far higher quantities than any Western numeric system, making them "surely peerless among the nations."[42]

As the year 1940 approached Japan prepared a great celebration of the 2600th anniversary of the nation's founding, planning to host the Olympics, the World's Fair, and year-long festivities for all the nations. Sakai, though, felt a deep sense of foreboding, and openly spoke of that year as "Armageddon" and "the end of days," which bordered dangerously on treason despite his careful formulation of Armageddon as a neutral, transformative event. In fact, Japan grew increasingly isolated due to its militarism and was unable to hold any international events in 1940. In June of that year Sakai ceased publication of his newsletter, citing the impending arrival of Armageddon, fell ill, and died in July. In 1941, having run out of options to fuel its military machine, Japan attacked Pearl Harbor and began the Pacific War.[43]

THE PUZZLE OF A METAPHYSICAL HISTORY

The Takenouchi Documents appear to fall into a class of parahistory different from those previously discussed in that evidence supporting them comes not only from the discovery of the true history of the world, but from cosmology, ultra-ancient archaeology, and even assurances from advanced beings from higher dimensions. As opposed to the *Kujiki-72, Hotsuma Tsutaye,* or Katakamuna Documents, where a metaphysical appeal is supported by linguistic beauty and uncovered philosophy, the Takenouchi Documents contain neither special linguistic traits nor an explicitly laid-out philosophy as such, but fit securely into a deeply symbolic traditional world that gives proponents the means to discover what is true and righteous.

Supernatural Experiences

The decision to research the Takenouchi Documents and spread the word about them appears to be inevitably based on a personal, spiritual experience. I do not know of any proponent for the Documents who did not report such an experience. Kiyomaro Takeuchi was commanded to distribute the Documents by a divinity.[44] His family also swears that his grandfather taught him a spell that gave him the ability to fly, and that he did this on rare occasions in their presence. This spell was not passed down to the current shrinekeeper.[45]

General Yutarō Yano's wife was possessed by a spirit who, writing on paper, demanded that he investigate what the spirit called "old documents of Tōryō Kōtai Jingū," explaining that this research would "cause a million things to begin." Yano and his wife were reportedly baffled by this message until their friend Sakai told them of the existence of the Takenouchi Documents and Kōso Kōtai Jingū, which they had never heard of before.[46] (Why the spirit wrote Tōryō 棟梁, meaning *pontifex maximus,* instead of Kōso 皇祖, "imperial ancestors," is unclear.) Sakai himself was, of course, guided by his vision of the Sun Cross.

Kiku Yamane says that in 1936, before she knew anything about the Takenouchi Documents, she had a dream about Christ standing on the Bering Strait bathed in the light of the Sun, a dream so vivid she published it in a magazine. In retrospect she realized that "unbeknownst to me, I was being guided by the unseen spirit of Christ to step into the world of ancient literature research." Yamane additionally reports that Kiyomaro Takeuchi had a waking vision of Christ being concerned about his plans to preach the Documents to foreigners. Apparently the time was not right in the 1930s to reveal the story of Christ's grave to the outside world.[47]

In the postwar period Wado Kōsaka related climbing up a hill and crying in the direction of Mount Fuji: "Is is true what the Takenouchi Documents say? If so, I will devote all my life to prove the documents. If not, I will end up wasting my entire life. Please let me know the truth." In response he saw "a brilliantly shining golden ball," which flew directly toward him and spoke: "This is the true history. Rest assured in carrying out this research we in Heaven will protect you at all times. If you deviate, we will guide you to the right direction." Kōsaka felt certain he had just spoken to a high-level being.[48]

Mikoto Nakazono felt drawn to the twin megaliths "Jean and Jeanne," on the island of Belle-Île in France. When he arrived and prayed to the stones, he received messages from the Celtic ancestors who installed them, confirming and elaborating on the message of the Takenouchi Documents. The Celts said that they were one of the races who were given the Kototama Principle by the World-Emperors and that the Great Concealment was still going according to their ancient plan. The Celts, "as the first emissaries of [the Land of the Sun], were the first to realize the limitations of the spiritual civilization . . . a way had to be found to prove the existence of the Life Principle to the physical senses." Soon Nakazono realized that the history he was hearing, confirming the Takenouchi Documents, was not only spoken by the Celtic kami but was in fact a metaphysical truth echoed by many people from all ages.[49]

Author and researcher Professor Joscelyn Godwin wondered when reading the accounts of the lost continent of Mu why it was necessary to suppose the existence of texts at all if information can be directly retrieved from spiritual sources.[50] The anecdotes related here may clarify the matter. While the Documents exist in a world where non-human entities interact with humanity, there is clearly some purpose to the existence of a physical text, so much so that these entities direct us toward them.

Some Astounding Coincidences

The Takenouchi Documents do not skirt around the fact that they are the truth behind everything we see today, even to the point of stretching plausibility. In addition to the Christ and Moses stories they claim that modern cities such as New York, Boston, Johannesburg, and Sydney were named after vassals of the World-Emperors who lived millions of years ago. The proponents of the documents simply see these city names as self-evident proofs, even though they alienate those who are not of the proper inclination. It seems that proponents believe this to be just one of a large number of coincidences that match up the Documents with other sources of information, some of which I will now summarize.

As the dynasties passed from High Ancient to Fukiaezu to Kamu Yamato, the length of each era steadily decreased. In the earliest, longest eras the World-Emperor and his citizens could live for millions of years, but our latest, most degenerate age will also be the shortest and brings with it the shortest individual lifespans. This closely parallels the cycle of yugas in the Indian scriptures with our Kali Yuga being the shortest. But there is no evidence any of the Takenouchi Documents' proponents or researchers have been aware of the yuga cycle. The current shrinekeeper of Kōso Kōtai Jingū, the grandson of Kiyomaro Takeuchi, explains the shortening dynasty lengths by owing them to the increasing degeneracy of later ages but is unfamiliar with other world doctrines on the same subject.

The Documents describe the planet that the World-Emperors reigned over as being home to Five-Colored Peoples who were scattered haphazardly throughout each continent. They claim that these groups appeared simultaneously, coexisted for millions of years, and did not fight. Although some in the West, such as the Theosophists, had hypothesized races succeeding each other or fighting in the deep past, the first person to propose the simultaneous appearance of different races was Edgar Cayce in a reading in May 1925. Oddly Cayce also proposes five different races, which he says came into existence roughly ten million years ago.[51] Just three years later the Takenouchi Documents appeared, referring to Five-Colored Peoples that existed for millions of years, but Cayce was unknown in Japan until years after his death.

In the Far East the five colors of white, blue, red, yellow, and black have been grouped for thousands of years under the Wu Xing. They were not traditionally associated with groups of people. The term "five-colored peoples" first appeared in the Shintoist Tsunehiko Sano's book *Honkyō Shinri Shinan Zukai* (1883). Sano tells us in this work that he is merely conveying information about the origin of the races that has been transmitted from the distant past. Like contemporary esoteric writers in Europe he does not explain where he found this information.[52] It does not seem that he was drawing on any Chinese or Japanese source known to us. Rather it seems that his "ancient sources" necessarily share something in common with the Takenouchi Documents.

The Documents describe a world continuously rocked by catastrophes, the previously mentioned Tenpenchii. Decades after the

Takenouchi Documents appeared Immanuel Velikovsky, who could not be reasonably claimed to have known of them, developed his own theory that the Earth was subjected to constant catastrophes in the deep past. His historical methodology was viciously criticized, but we have to wonder what was incarnate in him that made him start looking for those ancient records of catastrophe.

The Takenouchi Documents are said to use over 2,000 different types of kamiyo moji, which are said to be the origin of all modern writing systems, not just modern Japanese. As they appeared in Japan, Ferdinand Ossendowski was claiming in the West that the King of the World used an ultra-ancient script called Vattanan. The Vattan script of the Kingdom of Agartha, home to the symbolic World-King, is referred to in the suppressed book *Mission de l'Inde* by Saint-Yves d'Alveydre. Although these are said to be the origin of writing, unlike the Takenouchi Documents, there are no books written in Vattan or Vattanan script.

Anyone who has read James Churchward's *The Lost Continent of Mu* will have noticed countless parallels to the Takenouchi Documents: rediscovered ancient documents telling of a completely forgotten Empire of the Sun, where distinct peoples and races were ruled under a single emperor, and of course sunken continents. There appear to be some geometric resemblances as well (fig. 4.6). But Churchward's book was not known in Japan until 1932, while the first of the Takenouchi Documents was released to a study group in 1928. Furthermore, writings of Churchward that were not published until 1997 also exhibit similarities to the Takenouchi Documents, such as a "tablet supposed to have been written by Moses." I have focused on Guénonian symbolism, but a full investigation of the Mu parallels could take up another chapter.[53]

Takenouchi and Other Parahistories

Proponents of other parahistories do not generally advocate for parahistory as a genre, seeing it as an impediment to getting their preferred document accepted by mainstream society. But Takenouchi researchers do look into other parahistories and find in them a verification of

Figure 4.6. From left to right: the Japanese chrysanthemum, symbol of the Emperor and of the World-Emperor in the Takenouchi Documents; the "Royal Escutcheon of Mu" from Churchward's book; Sakai's Sun Cross.

their narrative. The journalist Yasukazu Fuse examined the *Hotsuma Tsutaye* and discovered that it mentions some interesting details about Takenouchi no Sukune. It says that he was a great teacher who lived in Hokuriku and that he knew the secret to longevity. It also mentions that when Xi Wangmu came to Japan to receive teachings she went not to the capital but to that same Hokuriku region. Perhaps she was visiting Kōso Kōtai Jingū?[54]

Wado Kōsaka, for his part, discovered in the Katakamuna Documents a scientific method that was perfected by the ultra-ancient Japanese. He seemed to consider the Katakamuna Documents proof that the World-Emperors had perfected the ability to create life, neutralize radioactive elements, and make energy through cold fusion. Since the Takenouchi Documents already have over 2,000 different kinds of kamiyo moji, the Katakamuna Documents are just another kind from that era.[55]

IS THE WORLD-EMPEROR A NATIONALIST?

What kind of figure is a World-Emperor? Clearly his position has nothing to do with the political machinations of a modern dictator. One able writer summarized the greatest political thinkers of the twentieth century as follows: "According to both Raymond Aron and Hannah Arendt, total rule is essentially determined by the element of terror."[56] The political writing of Michel Foucault could be accurately summarized with a similarly dark message. Note the complete contrast between the Takenouchi World-Emperor and the terrifying villain constructed by these political philosophers. Modernity has allowed us to both fantasize and realize a false, counter-Traditional regime that spreads fear and lusts for infinite power. The Traditional ruler whose selfish desires are curbed and whose right and justice are real is now out of our reach and dismissed as fantasy, even though the universal existence of this symbol evidences its basis in true principles.

Katsutoki Sakai declared that "the Emperor cannot permit" being used as a political tool by any one group of people, and Wado Kōsaka repeats this admonition, but neither of these writers can stop the Takenouchi Documents from being smeared with the brush of politics. Modern Japanese academics have advanced an extremely cynical reading of the Documents, which depicts them as a power play for Japanese racial supremacy in an era of empire. Their grounds for this claim, basically, are that the documents depict a Japanese civilization of immense age with access to high technology, which ruled over the peoples of the world, taught writing to the Chinese, and so forth, *quod erat demonstrandum*.[57]

The laziness of this theory should be evident. Kiyomaro was prosecuted not once but twice by the national government for distributing the Documents, and authorities were infuriated by Kōso Kōtai Jingū's claim to have inherited the real imperial treasures and a secret history. As even the critic Akira Fujiwara notes, Western reporters found the story of Christ's grave a great source of amusement. Censored by the government, ridiculed by the world—you really could not imagine a worse justification for nationalism or supremacism.

The Takenouchi Documents undoubtedly employ the concept of the nation and exalt Japan's divine ancestry, but they are not at all nationalist in the sense of supporting the policies of the contemporary regime. One Takenouchi researcher, General Yutarō Yano, concluded that what was needed to decouple the Emperor from the political manipulators was a battle for spiritual goodness, even one that could cause civil war and natural disasters in Japan, before a truly peaceful world federation could begin. Furthermore, after a close analysis of ultra-ancient maps, he announced that Japan was wrong to occupy Korea since it was not Japanese territory! Yano was arrested for having defamed the imperial history and promoted a "spirit geneaology," and he died in prison.[58]

Skeptics paint Yano as an ultranationalist, but they do not explain how a patriot could be arrested for *lèse-majesté*. Clearly Yano was not a very good ultranationalist if he wanted Japan to surrender its colony in Korea. Are we to regard him as having "misread" the documents? How can a "correct" reading be determined at all outside of one's personal convictions? The authorship of the Takenouchi Documents is unknown, so not even learned scholars can know the intentions of the authors. What we have concrete evidence for, and can easily determine, are the actions taken by believers in the Takenouchi story, an immense group of people that includes not only military generals and adventurers but also artists, writers, religionists, and historians. Mimura Saburō (1904–1975) documented the positive influence of the Documents on these people in books like *Japan and Israel: Enigmas of the World* (1950), but there is one story that he and other researchers have overlooked, which demonstrates more than any other the real power of the documents.[59]

The Japanese Moses and the Manchurian Jews

In 1935 General Jinzaburō Masaki paid several visits to Norihiro Yasue, the aforementioned Judaism expert who has been described by historian Ben-Ami Shillony as a "pragmatic military man," and who was then a lieutenant colonel in the Japanese Army. What he records in his diary is quite interesting: Yasue was engaged in intense research of the Takenouchi Documents throughout that year and chattered eagerly not about the army, but about the Documents. During his first visit in April, General Masaki simply cautioned Yasue not to go around speaking blasphemies against the imperial family. Masaki returned in June and this time Yasue wanted to tell him about the discovery of Moses's grave in Toyama prefecture. Finally, Masaki visited once more in September, and this time was informed about Jesus's arrival in Japan—Yasue had visited the Aomori grave in person and had come back with a glowing impression.

The irritated General Masaki finally told Yasue to cease his idle researches and return to the pressing questions of the day, such as the delicate administration of the Imperial puppet state Manchukuo.[60]

Two years later, Norihiro Yasue made connections in the Manchurian Jewish community to encourage them to keep living there, even as conditions for Jews worsened in Russia and Nazi Germany. He conducted official surveys of their community to ensure they were treated well by their neighbors. Countering the anti-Semitic propaganda spread by the Nazis, and even rebuffing a Nazi butcher who personally came to Shanghai with poison gas to use on the Jews, Yasue and others reminded military officials of Japan's official commitment to racial equality, and as a result the lives of the Jews were protected as well as anyone could be during such a horrific war.

In total, about 24,000 Jews survived the Holocaust by coming to Japan, including several Eastern European *yeshivot*—that is to say, entire schools of Jewish law were saved by rescuing students and teachers alike from mass murder. When the Soviets approached Manchuria in 1945 the majority of Yasue's comrades hurried onto boats back to Japan, or took their own lives rather than surrendering. Instead of joining them Yasue wrote a letter to his family expressing his feelings of responsibility for the war, handed himself over to the invading army, and died in a labor camp in 1950.

The simplistic story believed by many, including much of the Jewish community, is that Yasue was influenced by the anti-Semitic *Protocols of the Elders of Zion,* another forgery with a huge psychic impact, and even that the Japanese in general naively accepted Nazi stories of Jewish world domination. However Yasue read the *Protocols* in 1922 and by the 1930s he was no longer telling friends about the *Protocols* and clearly did not believe that Jewish people were evil. Because his biography is so complex Yasue's intense researches into the Takenouchi Documents in 1935 have been completely ignored. According to these documents, as explained above, the laws of Moses and Jesus are founded in the ancient teachings of the Japanese emperors, and therefore the faithful of the world are expressing oneness in spirit with a long-lost true Japan. The

Documents that Yasue read bring the message of Japanese history into a mythical union with the universal harmony preached by other great teachers, affirming the value of truths he had known all along.

Conclusion

Critics of the Takenouchi Documents have asserted that its usurpation of the source of all teachings in Japan is mere arrogance, and in some aspects its superficial message is unbelievable, but I believe the traditional parallels demonstrated by Guénon show that the idea of a Holy Land from which teachings come, ruled by a World-Emperor, is not idiosyncrasy but the discovery of a deeper truth. This is the same truth that tells us of Emperor Barbarossa sleeping beneath Kyffhäuser, of Utnapishtim waiting at the end of the world, of King Arthur returning to save his kingdom, of the Redeemer, the Mahdi, and countless others. Nor is this a nationalist legend. Adherents believe in a New Age of world peace when the myths of Japan will be reconciled with the faiths of the world, but that this New Age requires a spiritual understanding of the World-Emperor, a symbol that they believe is still present, but concealed, all over the world.

Guénon closes *The King of the World* with a warning that "events unfold with such rapidity" in the modern, technological age "that many things, the reasons for which are not immediately obvious, could well find rather unforeseen applications." He tells us he wishes to avoid direct "prophesying," but clearly he believes that the doctrine of the King of the World has some pertinence to our modern situation. In place of a straightforward prophecy he quotes a French monarchist saying that "we must be ready for an immense event in the divine order, which we are traveling toward with an accelerated speed."[61] Closing his *Sacred Symbols of Mu,* James Churchward asks us: "What is to be the end of this present civilization?" Meanwhile Wado Kōsaka, referencing the *Hitsuki Shinji,* says that we are fast approaching the "Age of Miroku" when the World-Emperor will once again be needed, and for which the Takenouchi Documents serve as a guidepost.[62] Why were these legends revealed in the twentieth century, and what sort of "immense event" are they pointing us toward?

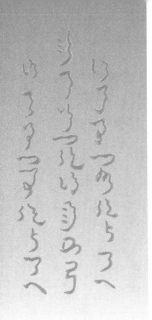

5
Ancient Science for Modern Mystics

The Katakamuna Documents

Science or magic? Readers inquiring into the nature of the Katakamuna Documents will have to transcend this dichotomy if they hope to understand the "experiential physics" described in its spiral shaped "eight-mirrored script" because it never sinks to the mundane realm of Newtonian mechanics. Several commentaries offer attempts to explain what Katakamuna means for the layman, but it appears impossible to discuss the content of these documents without scrambling your writing into obscure, esoteric vocabulary and strange neologisms. One commentator covers his book in medieval alchemical illustrations, references G. I. Gurdjieff and Goethe, and compares a cyclotron to the shape of a horsetail as part of his attempt to expound the meaning of the documents. Another commentary explains the light that Katakamuna throws on Theosophy, embryology, and ancient Chinese philosophy. These writers without exception translate the documents themselves using several different levels of explanation and provide commentaries to draw out the intended message.

It seems that what we are dealing with here is not really a science in the common, phenomenological sense, but a *sacred science* in the sense

128

of the great perennial thinker René Guénon: a method of drawing out deeper meaning from the symbols that constitute the world, not a limited "philosophy" or "system" but a truly all-encompassing knowledge.[1] The word science was used for many centuries to describe various kinds of knowledge, including the meditative practices of alchemy, astrology, and theurgy. Guénon believed, looking at Hermetism and the Indian yogas, that he was describing a perennial knowledge with origins in an era where radically different worldviews made such knowledge possible. Can one really claim that the Katakamuna Documents, which were allegedly written in ancient times but first appeared in 1966, fall into the same category?

Guénon's description of the form and function of sacred science should be useful here in helping us classify a kind of document rarely found in Japan. The Katakamuna mystery is a difficult case to crack, but perhaps this reading will suggest that the Japanese writers who take on the challenge of Katakamunan science are correct to analogize it with other kinds of sacred quests. The most notable sources here are *The Mysterious Katakamuna Civilization* (1981), by an esotericist with the pseudonym Akiyoneto (the Japanese rendering of the Chinese transliteration of "Archimedes"), and *The Road to Katakamuna* by Jirō Sekigawa and Yoshihiro Inada (2009).

WHAT THE ENGINEER FOUND IN THE MOUNTAINS

The content of the Katakamuna Documents is mixed up with the life of Satsuki Narasaki (fig. 5.1), who brought them to the world's attention. His biography is well documented, but his way of thinking remains enigmatic. He was by all accounts an ordinary engineer for the first half of his life, researching coal liquefaction and ironworking until hired by the Kwantung Army, a division of the Japanese Army that had recently invaded and subjugated Manchuria. He was assigned to a secret project in the Manchurian city of Jilin, officially called an iron foundry, but which was also doing some other kind of work that he cryptically

Figure 5.1. Satsuki Narasaki (1899–1974).

referred to as "mass power." His daughter believed that atomic energy was involved, but all records of this unit were destroyed in 1945. The only reliable information we have is that Narasaki's inventions were so treasured by Prime Minister Hideki Tōjō that they were declared state secrets.[2]

When Narasaki repatriated from Manchuria after World War II he started promoting something called *plantwave agronomy* to farmers in his area, which he claimed would revitalize plant cells by pumping them with waves of electric potential. He was soon employed by a small company, Hoshi Pharmaceuticals. Hoshi happened to be run by the father of the famous science fiction author Shin'ichi Hoshi, who reported that Narasaki was constantly promoting the use of electric currents to improve the taste of food and liquor and make it more healthful.

In 1948 Narasaki left Hoshi and began an epic quest to measure the electromagnetic fields of all Japan, which resulted in the discovery of a parahistory. Rather than publish his findings immediately, though, he kept the documents secret for seventeen years, slowly deciphering them based on his own methods. Meanwhile, for a bizarre period in the early 1950s plantwave agronomy became entangled in a three-way battle for the hearts of Japan's farmers against the Japanese Communist

Party's *Lysenko agronomy,* a Soviet alternative science that focused on hybridization, and the Church of World Messianity's *Avalokiteśvara agronomy,* which was basically organic farming and is still advertised today under the name "nature farming."[3]

Narasaki was also inventing his own form of science based on the parahistory's scientific system, which he published in 1958 as *Three Statoelectric Laws,* which are the laws of plants, materials, and humanity. This book is extremely hard to read because many of its technical terms are not standard Japanese but are compounds of unusual words or are neologisms that have been assigned a special meaning by the author. We lack an understanding of why Narasaki's 1958 *Three Statoelectric Laws* fails to mention the Katakamuna Documents. Even as he asserts that the ancient Japanese had an intimate knowledge of particle physics, he attributes this to his own interpretation of the *Kojiki* and *Nihon Shoki.*[4]

With regard to plantwave agronomy, in the February 2006 issue of *Agricultural Manager,* Yoshihiro Gotō interpreted *Three Statoelectric Laws* as saying that a conducting material should be inserted into the soil. He thus laid carbon into the ground underneath a buckwheat field that had not been growing well and was surprised to discover lively and uniform growth. This intriguing result has not yet been verified by other independent researchers but suggests that Narasaki's research may offer improvements for natural science.[5]

Narasaki began to discuss his Katakamuna discovery in 1966. A modern, postwar parahistorian, he seemed to doubt his own memory and the reliability of his senses, but he stuck to the truth of this story, and unlike Katsutoki Sakai, was consistent in his teaching throughout his life. Narasaki's story, as he told it, is as follows.

A Stranger in the Woods

The year was 1949. Still under American occupation, Japan was emerging from the ruins of a horrific war. Scientists in this era were familiar with harsh conditions. In the mountains of Hyōgo prefecture, Satsuki Narasaki set out into the wilderness with a team of assistants aiming to measure the electromagnetic field of the Earth in an undisturbed place. He came across a little hill named Fox's Mound and set up a lean-to there. He laid out wires and devices to measure the tremors and currents in the area and slowly began his painstaking measurements.

In January 1950 a middle-aged hunter came by Narasaki's encampment. "What do you think you're doing here?" he asked. "There are foreign objects in the river, and the animals can't drink. Take them out." Narasaki did as he said and removed the wires and devices.

The next day the hunter returned bearing a bundle of scrolls under his arm. "You guys have done good," he said. "To thank you, I'll let you take a look at these." He offered the scrolls to Narasaki. There were eighty different documents written on crumbling paper several centuries old. The script was not Japanese but a series of spirals made up of circles and crosses.

The hunter introduced himself as "Right Cross" (Hira Tōji) and claimed that his father was the shrinekeeper of Katakamuna Shrine, which was somewhere deep in the mountains. The scrolls were the ancient treasure of the Katakamuna kami, and an ancient taboo said that anyone who unrolled them would go blind. Nevertheless Right Cross said he had tried to show them to a professor, only to be told they were old family crests or drawings of sword helms. This annoyed the hunter and he asked Narasaki to prove those scholars wrong. Examining the documents for himself, Narasaki was surprised to realize that not only were they a definite script, but that he knew what the name of the script was.

When Narasaki was researching iron production in Manchukuo in 1941, an unusual thing had happened to him. One day, acting on a request from the Manchurian ironsmiths, he canceled work for a day so they could attend a festival at a Taoist mountain temple some miles to the south and decided to go along with them to see what it was about. Leaving the security of the colonial city behind, he observed the festivities at Mount Běishān and donated a fair amount of money, which surprised the temple's abbot so much that he was invited to come inside (fig. 5.2). He was the first Japanese ever to step foot inside the temple. The abbot,

Figure 5.2. The Taoist temple in Manchuria where Satsuki Narasaki discovered the secret of ultra-ancient ironworking.

Master Lú Yōu Sān, invited him in and served him a cup of tea from a strange iron kettle that he warmed to boiling with just a handful of small leaves.

Narasaki took a great interest in this kettle. He praised the ingenuity of Chinese ironworkers, and when he went back to Jilin that evening he could not get the mystery of the kettle out of his head. The next day he returned to the temple and asked where he could find such marvelous iron. The master explained it was a secret, but that the kettle had been bought in Japan long ago. Narasaki went home defeated, but stubbornly attempted to return to the temple a third time. His frustrated translator at this point no longer wanted to come along, so knowing no spoken Chinese, Narasaki took pen and paper with him to communicate with Master Lú through the kanji characters used in both Japan and China. The master was at first resistant, but after a silent argument was scratched out on paper he revealed a shocking secret of unbelievable magnitude.[6]

Thousands of years before the Stone Age, said Master Lú, an ancient tribe called Asiya lived on the Japanese islands. The Asiya wrote in what he called the Eight-Mirrored Script and had an advanced understanding of topics such as medicine, nuclear physics, and the meaning of life, in fact a more complete knowledge than any modern human being. The iron in the kettle had been made using their special processes. The ancient teachers and philosophers of China did their best to convey the tradition from Japan, but the knowledge of the Asiya's existence was never put to paper and only transmitted in secret. Narasaki became the first and only Japanese person to learn of this secret history.

Narasaki instantly recognized the script of the Katakamuna Shrine's documents in a flash of insight, and begged Cross to lend him the scrolls. As they were betrothed by the kami to Katakamuna Shrine, Cross could not let the scrolls out of his sight. But he allowed Narasaki to transcribe the spiraling words of the Eight-Mirrored Script into his research notebook over the course of one month, and occasionally talked with him about the texts' provenance. Narasaki returned from the mountain with a new gift for the world, if anyone would believe him.

If you felt like this story resembles a fairy tale more than any kind of real occurrence, you are not alone. Right Cross is obviously not a real name, but rather parallels the right crosses found in the Eight-Mirrored Script. No evidence has been found for the existence of a shrine named anything like Katakamuna. None of Narasaki's assistants from this expedition have been located, although anecdotal evidence suggests he was in the mountains at that time. But unlike the researchers of the Takenouchi Documents, who frequently have their parahistory's veracity affirmed by personal visions and extra-dimensional sources, those who study Katakamuna stick closely to the facts, and simply acknowledge the unusual nature of the story.

What is odd is that even Narasaki himself did not seem to believe that the "hunter" was a real person. Rather, he believed that he had somehow encountered an intellectual principle common to the authors of all the Japanese histories and parahistories. "We might say that the *Kojiki* and *Nihon Shoki* were also a response to 'Katakamuna,' by the Japanese of 2000 years ago," he said. "The *Uetsufumi* [a parahistory; see appendix A] was an interpretation by one person 800 years ago. And, with this reading, I am offering my response as a modern, twentieth century Japanese."[7]

René Guénon examined the similar problem of the Mimāmsā hermeneutics of the ancient Indian Vedas, which are attributed to unknown and opaquely named writers, and concluded that its authors were not meant to be real personalities at all. "It is easy to see," he wrote, "that it is not a historical or legendary person we are dealing with in this instance, but a genuine 'intellectual function,' amounting, one may say, to a permanent function." In fact, the *Right Cross* is an intellectual concept valued quite highly by Guénon—one of his principal works is entitled *The Symbolism of the Cross*. The equation of a teacher or messenger to a principle, as Narasaki has done, evidences a worldview where eternal knowledge is not conveyed by overtly supernatural means, but by private, esoteric means that can only be explained to the world through a patently strange story like this.[8]

Even in the modern era Narasaki was not the only one to tell his story in this fashion. Carlos Castaneda, whose book *The Teachings of Don Juan* appeared two years after Narasaki's and with much greater fanfare, faced similar skepticism from close readers. Like Narasaki, Castaneda met a mysterious man nobody else has ever seen who came from a place nobody else has confirmed to exist, and both presented the world with secret knowledge from this unlikely source—although Castaneda's story was outrageous and controversial, mass marketed in paperback form, while Narasaki's is oblique and circulated only in a small, self-published journal. Those who wish to learn from these teachers must figure out a way to make sense of the stories of how they got their knowledge.

If Narasaki's author was an intellectual function, how did it find him in the wilderness? In a posthumuous examination of his journals, researchers discovered that Narasaki had a hunch about this himself. During his time in the wilderness, he writes, he laid an offering to the fox spirit at the foot of Fox's Mound several times, only to see it disappear before his eyes. Eventually he asked Right Cross about this strange phenomenon. "Oh, that was me," said the hunter.

"But I didn't see you there!" Narasaki exclaimed.

"If you'da just looked closer," grumbled Cross mysteriously.

In his diary, Narasaki wondered whether Cross might be a fox, since the Japanese fox spirit behaves in this way. But esotericist Akiyoneto suggests a different story. According to the journal of the Narasaki Institute, Cross appeared one day and suddenly started talking about how the patriarch of the Katakamuna Shrine family, Dōan Ashia, did battle with the ancestors of the Japanese imperial family and fled to Kyushu. Recall Master Lú's mention of an Asiya tribe. The same journal claims that the fox's mound was held to be the grave of a Heian period sorcerer named Dōman Ashiya, an acknowledged but mysterious historical figure who might be called the Japanese Merlin. Akiyoneto believes it possible that Right Cross was himself the spirit of this Dōman Ashiya.

The Documents Are Released

As a result of close study of the Katakamuna Documents Narasaki gained a superior understanding of his own emotions and behavior. It is said that while ninety-nine out of one hundred incidents in Narasaki's life went smoothly, in that remaining one out of one hundred he could sense something uncomfortable and different, which prevented him from living in self-satisfaction. According to the teachings of ancient Katakamuna this was a type of resonance or vibration with the unseen world, called *kamikatari*. This one in one hundred was scarcely noticeable in material life but was in fact the power that lay above and ruled over the material world. (This bears an odd resemblance to the *Hitsuki Shinji*'s use of the terms "ninety-nine of one hundred" and "one of one hundred" to refer to things seen and unseen.)[9]

In 1966 Narasaki launched a journal called *Sōjishō* 相似象, a word of his own invention, which describes the phenomenon of physical things taking on resemblances to each other. In this private journal Narasaki began to propound the teachings he had discovered in the Katakamuna Documents, but he did not release his notebook at first. Instead he released a set of poems he had received through the close interpretation of his own "resonances" called the *Kamuhibiki,* "echoes of the kami."

From 1970 to 1973 Narasaki published 104 short poems under the title Kamuhibiki divided into thirteen categories ranging from *cosmic understanding* to *geonomy, agronomy, dendronomy,* and *laws of clothing manufacture*[10] that are valued equally with the Katakamuna Documents themselves. In 1970 he appointed a woman named Tamie Uno as his successor, and when he died in 1974 she took over publication of *Sōjishō.*

Uno was well studied in Mahayana Buddhism and, interestingly, Goethe. She was probably one of only a handful of Japanese people who have ever learned about Goethe's attempt to develop a different approach to science. It was Goethe who first identified *homology,* non-evolutionary resemblances between different life-forms, in his *Metamorphosis of Plants* (1790), but the mainstream scientific world overlooked his work. Narasaki had found a more than capable successor in Uno, for the word *sōjishō* appears to carry precisely the meaning of homology and Narasaki's attempt to describe a different kind of science is a direct parallel to Goethe.

Uno published Narasaki's notebook in 1979 and released additional material about how he had discovered the Katakamuna Documents and Eight-Mirrored Script. Like Narasaki, she did not widely publicize the discovery of the Documents, but only distributed her self-published journal to a growing number of interested readers. Over 1997–2003 she began to explain the meaning of each of the poems, but in 2006 she and her husband suddenly died in a house fire, and *Sōjishō* ceased publication.[11]

WORDS OF POSSIBILITY

The Katakamuna Documents are not just a matter of reading the claims within the text, or even listening to them as poetry. We must understand the language spoken by the ancient Katakamunan people, in which every syllable is imbued with meaning in kotodama style. The poems are meant to awaken one's inner sense of creativity, so reading them is more than just putting the teacher's thought into the disciple's head but is a matter of looking into the origins of every word to encourage interpretation, inspiration, and discovery. The first poem of the Documents proper runs like this:

katakamuna hihiki manosuheshi
ashiatouan utsushimatsuru
katakamuna utahi

Figure 5.3. The first poem of the Katakamuna Documents.

No simple translation can be made for this poem, but I can provide a definition of each syllable and element, after which the reader can reexamine the poem: Our world of forms (*kata*) is differentiation (*ta*) of energy (*ka*), which we know to be derived from essence (*kamuna*), the energy (*ka*) of qualitative (*mu*) Being/Name (*na*). The limitless, immaterial kamuna behind kata now resonates (*hihiki*). This resonation awakens us to "the power to get ourselves in tune with the force that controls change in the universe-sphere" (ma-no-suheshi). The resonance is a a song (*utahi*), a creation (*hi*) of differentiation (*ta*) of the reception of essence (*u*). Representing (*tsushi*) the reception of essence (*u*) through this song, and protecting (*tsuru*) the method of this reception (*ma*), Ashia Touan transcribes (*u-tsushi*) and honors (*ma-tsuru*) the *Utahi of Katakamuna.*[12]

As we can see here, every syllable of every word of Katakamunan Japanese corresponds to a specific concept in *intuitive physics,* and when we combine some of those forty-eight syllables to make a new word they interact with each other in interesting ways. Some of these words still exist in modern Japanese, for example *na* for name, *kata* for form, *utsushi* for transcription, and *matsuru* for sanctification. By taking apart these words we realize that while we simply think of a concept like *matsuru* as a primitive practice of religious worship, it once signified the need to protect the methods by which our ancestors received power from the dimension of Essence. Other concepts, like *ta* and *mu*, have been forgotten in modern Japanese, which is why it is important for people to understand the origin of Japanese in Katakamunan.

The Cosmic Eight-Mirrored Script

The Eight-Mirrored Script in which the Katakamuna Documents were written contains forty-eight syllables made entirely of circles and chords, corresponding to the sounds of ultra-ancient Japanese. As shown in figure 5.3 it is not written in straight lines, but spirals out from the center of the page. I know of no other script like it in the world.

At this pivotal center of the Eight-Mirrored Script lies one of three symbols that carry cosmological rather than linguistic meaning, symbolizing the source of inspiration from which the poem arises. The most common symbol is called the *Yatanokakami,* a symbol of the ancient, sacred treasure of the Japanese Emperor, which is usually called the Yata-no-Kagami (the Eight-Hand Mirror). The turning motion emanating from the central wheel of the imperial Yatanokakami recalls the King of the World, which in Sanskrit is *chakravartin,* "he who makes the wheel turn."[13]

The more obscure aspects of the Yatanokakami are the division of this wheel into four parts and the eight equally spaced small circles that intersect the large circle. Uno explained the meaning of these symbols by breaking down the Yatanokakami into its component characters in the Eight-Mirrored Script. These characters suggest their own kind of Hifumi Song, a song of creation similar to that of the *Kujiki*-72. The Yatanokakami appears when they are combined. She asks us to imagine the symbol as a kind of landscape:

> If we consider the horizontal line of the Yatanokakami, which indicates the origin of the sundry phenomena of this world, as a horizon line, then the vertical line is a person standing in the middle and observing. Light rises up from the East, the upper half indicates Noon, and the lower half Night. Therefore in the [Katakamunan] *hifumi* song—*hifumiyoi mawaritemekuru munayakoto* (a haiku, literally "1 2 3 4 5, turning and rotating, 6 7 8 9 10")—hi is the east (*higashi*) where light comes from. It passes one by one through the syllables of day *fumiyoi,* representing what is seen, turning as it rotates, and passes into the syllables of night *munayakoto,* representing the unseen. Everything in the universe, from the biggest galaxy to the smallest particles, possesses a ball-nature (*mari*) dependent on its rotation (juncture) and circulation (revolution) between darkness and light. It goes without saying that *hifumiyoi munayakoto* is a sequence from 1 to 10.[14]

This does seem to reflect the shape of the characters *hi, fu, mi, yo, i* which look like a sun moving from east to west across a sky, and *mu, na, ya, ko,* to which show an orb completing this circle underneath the "horizon." Note that six and seven, the most magical numbers in Western numerology, are in Katakamunan Japanese mu and na, respectively "quality" and "Being/Name," both applicable to ka-mu-na, power drawn from the world of essence that exists "behind" the visible world. The combination of all ten numerals is the Yatanokakami at the center of most of the poems.

THE MEANING OF THE NUMBERS
IN KATAKAMUNAN JAPANESE

NUMBER	CHARACTER	SYLLABLE	MEANING
1		hi	creation
2		fu	reproduction, or growth
3		mi	manifestation, or physical quality
4		yo	passing, or change
5		i	location
6		mu	essential quality
7		na	Being, or Name
8		ya	stability, balance, or limit
9		ko	circle, or revolve
10		to	synthesis, unification, or dissolution

The other two central symbols appear more rarely. Seven of the eighty poems have at their center a symbol called *Futomani,* said to symbolize the Imperial Grass-Cutting Sword, but which clearly recalls the ancient method of divination. Finally two of the poems, including the one quoted above, spiral out from an empty circle called the Mikumari, which is described as "the combination of all components and the origin of all things."[15] This clearly explained symbolism directly parallels the Western tradition of the "all-containing" sphere that can be dated back to Plato's Timaeus. In Guénon's estimation:

> The sphere, then, can be said to be the most universal form of all, containing in a certain sense all other forms, which will emerge from it by a means of differentiations taking place in certain particular directions; and that is why the spherical form is, in all traditions, that of the "Egg of the World," that is, the form of that which represents the 'global' integrality, in their first and 'embryonic' state, of all the possibilities that will be developed in the course of a cycle of manifestation.[16] [emphasis added]

According to Guénon the sphere and circle are symbolic of that which cannot be measured, in opposition to the angular forms of squares and cubes, which are the most specifically defined forms of manifestation and can be measured the most simply. This is borne out by mathematics insofar as the area of the circle and volume of the sphere can only be calculated by employing the irrational, *transcendental* number π, which in real engineering is only ever used in approximation. Therefore this Eight-Fold Script made of circle segments and chords is well suited to symbolize these higher concepts.

Spherical symbolism is a key element of both the script and the content of the Katakamuna Documents. The world of essence is defined as a *universe-sphere,* although Akiyoneto warns us away from thinking of this universe-sphere as a literal ball hanging in isotropic Cartesian space. Rather, *space* in the documents "is obviously quite a different thing from the space and time used in Newtonian thought," and readers are instructed to avoid imagining "a sequential, homogenous, isotropic, infinitely large Euclidean conception of space" or a linear flow of time.[17] Here again we are paralleling Guénon, who himself cautions that "Cartesian 'mechanism'" is insufficient to describe physical space because it assumes homogeneity.[18] Guénon warns his readers that the symbolism of the sphere is not a primitive reference to the Sun or any other spherical thing in the world, but points to a perfection that the Sun can only reflect.[19]

The Oldest Kind of Science

Although I dub the Katakamuna Documents "parahistory" because of their writing system and the way they were revealed to the world, the author or authors of the documents seem to take no interest in history whatsoever. Instead, their principal concern is *intuitive physics,* a reading of physics where conclusions are reached not through experiment but through intuitive understanding of the nature of the holistic universe. This use of the "scientific" word *physics* here may seem objectionable to modern readers, but in fact it was precisely physics that René Guénon intended to defend from scientism when he wrote:

> The term "physics," in its original and etymological sense, means precisely the "science of nature" without qualification; it is therefore the science that details with the most general laws of "becoming," for "nature" and "becoming" are in reality synonymous, and it was thus that the Greeks, and notably Aristotle, understood this science ... Already, therefore, one can see the significant deviation of meaning to which the modern world has subjected the word "physics," using it to designate exclusively one science among all others, all of which are equally natural sciences, and this is an example of that process of subdivision we have already mentioned as being one of the characteristics of modern science. This "specialization," arising from an analytical attitude of mind, has been pushed to such a point that those who have undergone its influence are incapable of conceiving of a science that deals with nature in its entirety.[20]

Although Guénon would balk at grounding his eternal truths in ephemeral neurological hypotheses, the psychologist Iain McGilchrist recently published a book on the hemispheric functioning of the brain, *The Master and His Emissary,* which makes precisely the same claim: the critical, analytic left brain has taken complete control of the post-Enlightenment intellect, and its relentless specialization shuts out the right brain's natural ability to interpret and harmonize. McGilchrist's claim is that Western civilization has fallen into "the hands of the vizier, who, however gifted, is effectively an ambitious regional bureaucrat with his own interests at heart. Meanwhile the Master, the one whose wisdom gave the people peace and security, is led away in chains."[21]

The real point of Guénon's criticism is to awaken us to the existence of this Master. Guénon does not question our knowledge of the mechanical forces by which objects affect each other. Indeed, he acknowledges that we have achieved a thorough understanding of these processes. But this limited, mechanical system of Newton's is encroaching on the ancient Greek term φυσικός (physikos), which encompasses all the activities of the natural world. The Japanese word for physics is *butsuri* 物理, the "nature of things," which raises the same issues. Aristotle's physics not only describes the cause of a ball rolling downhill, but also the cause of a person going for a walk, and unifies both of these complex activities in a single physical system.

Katakamuna physics, rather than continuing this narrow study of homogenous and indeterminate "matter," attempts to set up a language for Aristotle's more intuitive questions about human intellect and other matters of will. All commentators agree that "Katakamuna science studies the entire universe, while modern science studies only a part."[22] In fact, Akiyoneto's argument in *The Mysterious Katakamuna Civilization* is almost indistinguishable from Guénon:

> What is this thing that we call science, objectively verifiable science? People called scientists take readings from precisely quantified instruments in controlled experimental settings, and apply

deeply idealistic mathematics to them—nothing more than this. You lose contact with the outer world of your eyes and ears and fingertips.[23]

According to Jirō Sekigawa, Katakamuna physics is not a rigid system nor a religion but is a language to develop one's inherent intellectual capacities, which can be developed or improved upon by anyone. Indeed, in the Katakamunan language, the word for physics is *satori,* meaning "understanding" in modern Japanese, and this understanding we seek "does not deny the intellect but aims to properly grow the intellectual functions," so that we might be delivered from our confusion and gain a proper understanding of the world (*ma-no-suheshi*).[24]

The Language and Meaning of Katakamuna

The most important product of Katakamuna research so far has been to realize a symbolic language by which initiates organize intellectual concepts and connect them to each other. Guénon warns us that a true sacred science is not a "system." Thinking of it as a language, an ultra-ancient liturgical tongue, may be helpful. Unlike a perfected and closed system, in a language new words might be introduced, or old words slowly refined, but by and large the same concepts are being conveyed.

The redefinition of the world around us in Katakamuna terms begins with our concept of the *universe.* In the Katakamunan worldview the observable universe is just one half of Creation. The other half is the unseen world of essence against which the visible world exists in a state of opposition. When these worlds interact, in a process called *amautsushi,* the reaction gives birth to new life, thought, art, or any kind of creative thing. In modern Japanese amautsushi means "receiving from the heavens."

There are two ways for a human society to orient itself toward awareness of amautsushi. The first is to demean it as the private experiences of individuals and shut it out of everyday life. This is the way followed by modern civilizations, which Sekigawa says are "oriented toward the downfall of humanity." Such civilizations suppress our natural instinct toward the supermaterial world, but because that world rules over the material world these cultures are bound to eventually collapse out of their own ignorance and thoughtless "opposition."

The Katakamunans, on the other hand, embraced amautsushi and tried to make it part of their everyday lives, which were full of resonances received from the supermaterial world and transformed into creative power. Therefore, they called their nation *kata-kamu-na: kata,* "form" or "formed from," *kamu,* "essential," and *na,* "names" or "principles." Modern Japanese people are not aware of it, says Sekigawa, but it was their own ancestors who possessed this knowledge, and the modern language is full of survivals from that time. "The Japanese people originate from a society that was 'properly facing,' and the high ancient language of that origin's progenitors, the kami, is still being used today."[25]

What was life like in the Katakamunan world? The Documents themselves contain no historical information so we don't know much about their authors and their culture. Presumably, living tens of thousands of years ago, they were hunter-gatherers. But we know their descendants are the modern Japanese because they determined the locations of their festivals and gatherings by seeking out good places, called *iyashirochi,** for living things to naturally receive amautsushi, and these iyashirochi hotspots are now the locations of Japan's oldest shrines. Also, those high ancient people have left the Japanese with physical symbols of the proper understanding of the universe in the form of the Three Imperial Treasures.[26]

According to Sekigawa modern people can only conceive of space as "an empty expanse of nothing," but this is our own imagining. In the Katakamunan language *tokoro,* or space, is filled with *ma* (literally "openings," but used in modern Japanese to mean something like "opportunities," like *ma ni awanai* "I won't have the chance"). Time, *toki,* is filled with *i-ma* (moments) in the same way. Therefore, all places

---

*The word *iyashirochi* can be broken down in modern Japanese as *ii yashiro chi*—"good place for a shrine." It also contains the word *iyashi,* which means relaxation and healing.

and times are openings and moments by which amautsushi might be let in, if we can only become aware of it.[27]

The way to harness amautsushi is to escape from the tedium of the everyday into the immediacy of *now,* and then redirect that awareness of your present condition and behavior into your efforts. In our everyday lives we tend to tediously repeat the same actions over and over—this routine is precisely what must be overcome. "Taking as an example the homology demonstrated in animals molting and hatching, and flowers blossoming, we can make our hearts start *working* by escaping our old ways and matching up to the right 'resonances.' A few teachers, such as Buddha, Lao Tse, Christ, and Socrates, have been able to do this."[28]

The danger is that people are no longer aware of these residual traditions in their language, and are forgetting about the presence of *kamu,* unseen power. Already, Modern Japanese is full of imported words that do not carry the resonances of the original ancient tongue. Soon this material civilization will have to crumble, and a spiritual civilization will be built on its ruins; that future spiritual awakening will require us to get rid of these imported words. However, Sekigawa is not trumpeting any kind of nativism. He says that a "properly facing" civilization contains a culture of gentle, feminine yin (*awa*), while ethnic nationalism overly promotes solar and masculine yang (*sanuki*).[29]

All this is precisely as Guénon wrote. The tradition of past ages has today been "lost or hidden," but it lives on for a few who understand the way to open the gate: "their intention must be directed so that through the harmonic vibrations it awakens." Access to this knowledge is steadily weakening, "yet when this period comes to an end the tradition will be manifested anew in is integrality."[30]

Applied Intuitive Physics

The power of amautsushi, according to Katakamuna researchers, cannot be underestimated. Uno refers to it as "minus entropy," while Sekigawa calls it "the basic principle of creation." Even the creation of the world by Izanagi and Izanami is understood to be symbolic of great forces interacting. Narasaki makes the interesting claim in *Three Statoelectric*

Laws that the word *isa* once meant "particle," so keeping in mind the common words *nami* for wave and *nagi* for calm, the kami Izanami and Izanagi who gave birth to all worldly things symbolize "wave particles" and "calm particles," respectively.[31]

Over the course of his book Akiyoneto explores the physical possibilities of negative entropy, examining orgone energy, alchemy, and the work of French scientist Corentin Louis Kervran, whose radical hypothesis that biological processes can transmute elements has been confirmed by research done in the French Navy and U.S. Army, but has otherwise been ignored by the scientific community. Other writers theorize about picking up plus-ions out of the atmosphere among other ideas in order to tap into "space energy."[32] But this "principle of creation" can have other interpretations as well. It can refer to people's power to share thoughts through language, build culture and society together, and put creative energy into artwork and literature.

As every writer knows, creativity is not an easy thing to harness in a prolonged and reliable fashion. Amautsushi in general depends on local circumstances that our current, limited idea of science cannot properly predict. However, the Katakamunans passed down to us a science by which we might discover the geographical conditions for fertility, iyashirochi, and barrenness, *kegarechi*. Calculating the locations of iyashirochi in a field can help one determine where to plant crops, and the concept of iyashirochi has caught on in the Japanese New Age community as a local parallel to Chinese feng shui.

Akiyoneto, while mentioning feng shui and English ley lines, hones in on dowsing as the practice most closely related to iyashirochi, wondering whether Narasaki could have been describing the unseen and poorly understood process behind this highly successful activity. Akiyoneto claims that dowsers often feel as if they are getting in tune with natural patterns in the precise way suggested by intuitive physics. His apparent source is a 1975 British book, which says that "experienced dowsers, including . . . Guy Underwood, Reginald Smith and many others in Britain, have observed that every megalithic site is over a center or channel of the terrestrial current whose emanations are detected by the dowser's rod. All ancient tombs and stones were placed so as to coincide with and accumulate the flow of the earth's vital energy, its 'spirit.'"[33] Thus dowsing, ley lines, feng shui, and iyashirochi could be describing the same thing.

The concepts employed in the Katakamuna Documents, of energy with visible impact but invisible origin, have inspired many writers to deepen their understanding of the ancient principles of Jōmon era pottery, the workings of Chinese medicine, or the power of sacred mountains. These writers do not necessarily endorse the idea of a Katakamuna civilization, but they recognize that Narasaki and Uno tapped into some kind of knowledge not available from other sources.

René Guénon was picky with his sources of inspiration, rejected most modern claims to wisdom, and labeled Japan itself a "Western" nation in his *East and West* (1921). On the other hand though, as we saw in chapter 4, he was keen on reports of ancient wisdom received by modern people. It is hard to say what he would have thought about the Katakamuna Documents, but they do seem to parallel many of the terms he used to describe sacred science. Like his Heremitic and Vedic texts they alienate the great majority of readers, but provide to the few who are correctly inclined a powerful symbolic language by which one might come to understand the workings and the order of Creation.

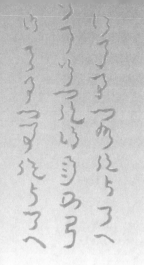

CONCLUSION

Parahistory and the Grey Gentlemen

Now, midway on our journey, we find ourselves in a forest dark. It is time for us to part ways, and yet we may be unsure of the purpose of all we have learned. To grow our understanding we need to know *why* these teachings come to us through this specific medium. Some probably already know the answer to this question, but many people will be confused and are in danger of being led astray, so I will do my best to clear things up on the assumption that elements of this book have been less than straightforward.

We have been examining texts of strange and ambiguous origin that assert they were issued from an ancient civilization otherwise unrecorded in history, and while some people probably think this makes perfect sense, for others there is an automatic reaction of "this is the mark of forgery," or "fakelore," or "mere religious fable." That reaction needs to be closely reconsidered. Does that really answer our question? What could possibly motivate an author, when he wants to convey an important message, to imitate the writing styles of earlier ages or even to invent new proto-languages, and thus make his work less believable and more confusing?

In parahistorical proposals, alternate histories are *inseparable* from metaphysical doctrines. Affirmations of one claim bolster the other. When skeptical groups analyze the documents, though, only historical claims are examined. These groups do excellent research, and we have referenced them in this book. But their attempts to explain *why* parahistory exists in Japan fall rather flat. Let us now examine the skeptical counterproposals and see how well they answer our question.

PARAHISTORY ON TRIAL

We have already seen how skeptics of parahistory engender a deep disdain for the Takenouchi Documents as the product of selfish nationalism, even though their wartime proponents not only harbored deep internationalist commitments but could also be quite heroic in their devotion, even resisting government pressure and censorship. It turns out that when it comes to determing the level of truth of parahistories, some of these skeptics have a declared double standard.

In a recent essay on parahistories for an academic publication, the skeptic Akira Fujiwara provides us with some of his personal thoughts on the subject of truth. With the case of the antiauthority parahistory *Tsugaru Soto Sangunshi* (see appendix A), which appeared in 1976 and basically claims that Tohoku had superpowered technology in ancient times and was subjugated by a tyrant calling himself Emperor, Fujiwara generously allows that even if the text is a forgery, it could still point to deeper truths. "I believe that there is another dimension beyond authenticity," he writes. "The important thing is to react to the historical fact of the existence of a forgery with the position that this must have been a manifestation of something in the spiritual world, and unearth the basis for the forgery." That is to say, the fabrication of one guy in 1976 might be echoing a cultural memory of some forgotten political events in Tohoku.

But Fujiwara is not so kind to texts like the *Kujiki*-72, *Hotsuma Tsutaye,* and Takenouchi Documents. These texts are to him pure fiction. Forgers of local history might be trying to relate historical truths, he says, but "in the case of the 'modern spurious national histories,' this does not apply . . . the 'modern spurious national histories' are simply fantasy. Even if one of the 'modern spurious national histories' were based on real folklore, one would find it utterly impossible to trace it to its original form."[1] What Fujiwara seems to be getting at is that it is impossible to find remnants of local rumors in nation and world-spanning parahistories like the Takenouchi Documents, which instead were made up from whole cloth, as it were, by their discoverers.

Now, this is very interesting. If we have established that something makes false claims, what sort of standard could make it true on a "higher level"? I would hold that a really true story relates true principles—to paraphrase G. K. Chesterton, fairy tales are true not because they tell us dragons are real, but because they tell us dragons can be beaten. In Fujiwara's world everything is upside down. He says that a really true story is one that is a distorted echo of some old, forgotten squabble. For him, fairy tales are true because the dragon might be a misremembered snake; the importance of defeating the dragon appears to be forgotten entirely.

According to Fujiwara's theory, local parahistories should provide the greatest truth and spiritual awakening, but this is not borne out by the facts: in reality, both skeptics and proponents are captivated by the tales of the Takenouchi Documents, the *Hotsuma Tsutaye,* and other national parahistories. If you visit a large Japanese bookstore it will be precisely these national "fantasies" that you see on the occult shelves, continuing to attract eager new students. Fujiwara does not even try to explain this. Perhaps these texts do provide a glimpse into the "spiritual world" and knowledge from "another dimension," to use his language.

What we have discovered about parahistory in this book totally undermines Fujiwara's philosophy. These texts were not produced with the intent of writing fiction, like an author might do if he were creating fantasy. They all resemble historical texts, and the authors make every appearance of recording a true forgotten history. So, assuming that none of them are ancient, why did their authors work so hard to make them look ancient? Do parahistories emanate from some true source, or are they a sign of malicious intent or mental illness? Are their proponents taking on the establishment, or do they suffer from naïveté or ignorance? Both Western and Japanese skeptics attempt to explain cases of ambiguous knowledge using a number of different labels, and proponents of these kinds of knowledge try to refute the labels. The argument over whether these labels apply can go on indefinitely without either side being convinced of anything. It needs to be transcended entirely because it does not touch the most important issues at hand. A quick survey of the most common labels will be proof enough of this.

Forgery!

The first and most obvious charge is that of forgery. Let us examine a recent instance where this charge was made. The prominent scholar Bart Ehrman has written an impassioned tract, *Forged* (2011), in which he claims that the Gospels would have been denounced as forgeries if the Church Fathers had only known that they were not actually written by Apostles. He complains several times that other biblical scholars have never looked at "what ancient people called this practice or considers what they had to say about it . . . they called books like this 'falsely inscribed writings,' 'lies,' and 'bastards'!"[2]

There is simply no way that what Ehrman writes is true—actually, I do not think Ehrman has thought this through very fully, because it is very funny to think about. Take the collective teaching of the Gospels, which remains amazing to us even today—Jesus overturning the tables of the moneylenders, washing the feet of his disciples, bearing his cross to his own grave—and go back in a time machine to tell the compilers of the New Testament, "Actually, you should denounce all of these accounts as forgeries and destroy all the copies, because the real disciples of Christ were probably illiterate." They would almost certainly look at you with pity.

Ehrman associates the *practice* of forgery with the *motive* of a "bastard text" written to disseminate lies for the author's personal gain. Certainly, there have been a few textual forgeries in recent times produced for monetary gain, like the Hitler Diaries that Ehrman cites, and Mark Hofmann's Mormon forgeries. The literary and philosophical worth of these is negligible; they appeared because the malicious forger realized that no matter what he produced, it would fetch a high price from historians trying to fill a gap in our knowledge.

But even in our own time, other people are producing pseudepigrapha for no personal gain whatsoever. Take for example the Majestic 12 documents, claiming to be evidence of a government conspiracy covering up extraterrestrial contact. The initial documents were probably part of a Cold War disinformation campaign, but decades after the end of the Cold War new materials continue to be "discovered" and uploaded to the Internet from unknown sources. Nobody can conceivably benefit from posting these texts anonymously and for free.

Even texts where the poison of material gain is involved seem to reflect deeper values. Every hoax is necessarily an imitation of a reality. Consider the *Dossiers Secrets d'Henri Lobineau,* which claim that a man named Pierre Plantard was to be the future Catholic King. Like the Takenouchi Documents, these documents are largely genealogical and range from mysterious and puzzling to unbelievable. They even fabricate a page from the journal *Regnabit* to which René Guénon contributed. These *Dossiers* opened up a tangled world of mystery surrounding Plantard's Priory of Sion, the book *Holy Blood, Holy Grail,* and the French village of Rennes-le-Château. The intrigue surrounding the *Dossiers* is ongoing as of this writing and would make an interesting comparison to these Japanese parahistories.

It seems that Pierre Plantard and his friends would have a simple motive for forging these documents, but we must remind ourselves that forging parahistorical genealogies is a very risky and unprofitable way to make a living compared to other unscrupulous lines of work. Fujiwara's views aside, when these world-spanning texts are created they reflect very deep desires on the part of the authors. The authors of the *Dossiers* are clearly quite dedicated to building up an esoteric mystery surrounding Christ, and the Takenouchi Documents are even more dedicated to supporting the Japanese imperial family, even at the expense of Kōso Kōtai Jingū's own claims to power. Even if these forgers were consciously appropriating little-known symbols for personal gain, their discovery and use of these symbols sheds deeper light on matters unrelated to the authors' own interests.

The other parahistories discussed in this book should clarify this matter further. There is very little motive to forge a seventy-two-volume text full of mystical and political teachings for the sake of one shrine, and no earthly motive can reasonably be established for the *Hotsuma Tsutaye* or Katakamuna Documents. I therefore find that the word forgery, even if it is applicable in a shallow sense, is just an excuse and carries no explanatory value. It does not actually tell us why parahistories were written—why it is that these writers with such an important thing to say are misdating their own writing.

Myth!

Next, consider Fujiwara's euhemerism, his belief that parahistory is valuable only insofar as it is a "code" for real historical data. This argument is timeless (its first proponent, Euhemer, was an ancient Greek) and has plenty of parallels in the modern West. Recently, Elizabeth and Paul Barber's well-researched book, *When They Severed Earth from Sky* (2006), endeavors to portray all human myth as an attempt to "encode" scientific information, and damns anyone who finds deeper symbolic meaning in myths as "prefer[ing] mystery and romance . . . to reasoned logic and careful evidence."[3]

This reduction of myths to nature is a myopic inversion of the mythmaking process at times, and simply falls short at others. Certainly it is clever to say that the story of Amaterasu in the rock cave helped the ancients remember how to respond to a solar eclipse, but J. R. R. Tolkien pointed out that the myth becomes something more than a mnemonic for its listeners when the personalities are added: "personality can only be derived from a person."[4] And what sort of natural event does the myth of Izanami and Izanagi refer to? Over 2,000 years ago Socrates responded to the original euhemerist by pointing out how many myths exist with no conceivable natural explanation: "Now I quite acknowledge that these allegories are very nice, but he is not to be envied who has to invent them; much labour and ingenuity will be required of him; and when he has once begun, he must go on and rehabilitate Hippocentaurs and chimeras dire."[5]

Like Socrates, we do not seek knowledge reduced to its lowest certainties, but knowledge raised to its highest possibilities. We do not want to be told what information can be confirmed by outside sources, but to know why there is so much information here that cannot be confirmed by anything else except our own convictions. So again, this word myth is not doing the job of explaining what is going on.

Allameh Tabatabaei, the great twentieth-century Islamic thinker, summarized the traditional view in saying that "for us the person who wrote the *Nahj al-Balaghah* is 'Ali even if he lived a century ago."[6] What did he mean by this? Clearly it was not that the author of the *Nahj* might have remembered some stray fragments here and there, which might have had their origin in 'Ali, or that the Allameh doesn't care about history in general. The truth and beauty of the *Nahj* is not founded on a historical claim; it is an eternal cornerstone of the tradition of 'Ali regardless of who wrote it.

Religion!

Even allowing that these texts were not produced to encode some material facts, or for material gain, we might wager that they were written for "religious" purposes. Look at how much they talk about heaven and Earth, and shrines, and even Jesus. Even though these are supposedly historical texts, it's a very common leap these days to assume that anything that humans do that does not fulfill animal needs of survival, sex, and power is a "religious delusion."

What does the word "religion" mean other than "untruth"— which begs the question of motive. Rather than explaining, this term only serves to obfuscate, especially in the context of Japanese history. Japan did not have a word translatable as "religion" until 1858 when the Americans coerced them into signing a document that guaranteed religious freedom.[7] At this point Buddhist temples became religious organizations, but shrines stayed the property of the government and were regulated as nonsectarian institutions open to all people, *as they always had been.* Even the esoteric currents mentioned in chapters 1 and 2 were unrelated to the general nonsectarian use of shrines.

The Japanese government maintained that their shrines were secular and public property until the Americans conquered them in 1945. At this point the arguments made by Christians, outlined in chapter 4, became government policy and the shrines were declared to have always been "religious," and were privatized as a religious corporation. He who claims that shrines were always religious is taking sides with the Christians and Americans against the Japanese.[8]

What does it mean that an activity that was once defined as secular became redefined as religious through a change of regimes? Was that activity never secular? Does it secretly remain secular? Someone would try to tell us that it must be one or the other, but who defines what activities are "religious" or "secular" other than a government? If it is the role of modern government to control and define the public sphere and relegate "religious" authorities to the private sphere, then is it in fact attempting to be the *single* source of *absolute* authority over public life, merely assuming the role of older sources of authority? As G. K. Chesterton said: "Once abolish the god, and the government becomes the god." Or as Professor Timothy Fitzgerald recently wrote,

> Is the Nation State (which nobody has ever seen) not a transcendental entity which receives regular ritual veneration from all branches of the establishment, live sacrifices in our war heroes, and arguably a form of worship by the whole nation at the Cenotaph in Whitehall in London? Is there an essential difference . . . between dying for one's country and dying for one's God?[9]

At the risk of repeating myself, it's not that the words forgery, myth, and religion *cannot* be applied; it's that these are excuses, and they explain very little, or nothing, about the meaning of these texts. They tell us about the circumstance and context of the texts, but they say nothing about the messages they convey to us. *Why did those messages choose this medium?*

PARAHISTORY AS TRUTH

Michael Ende, author of the internationally beloved children's book *The Neverending Story,* was once invited to a conference for managers and economists who had been discussing financial issues for several days. It was a little unusual, he realized, for a children's author to address a room full of businessmen. But he was interested to hear their answers to a simple, childlike question he had. He explained himself as follows:

> I'm concerned that in this century, we have seen few positive utopias. The last stories that even *intended* to be a positive utopia were written in the century before ours, such as Jules Verne, who believed that humans could truly live in happiness and freedom with the progress of technology, or Karl Marx, who thought that a socialist state could guarantee perfect happiness and freedom. We know now that those utopias were self-contradictory and mistaken. But the futures we have imagined in this century, from Wells' *Time Machine,* to Huxley's *Brave New World,* to Orwell's *1984,* are nothing if not nightmares. It's as if we have embraced an anxiety about our own futures. We feel so helpless that it seems like we really don't even know what we *hope* for any more. So, I have a proposal. We've been talking about today's problems all day long, so now let's get on a flying carpet and ride 100 years into the future. I'd like each of you to tell us what kind of world you'd *hope* to see there. [. . .] In other words, I'd like us to play a game. In this game, everyone has to say something. There's only one rule: nobody is allowed to say, "that's impossible." Other than that, say whatever you can think of. You can talk about an industrial society, or a society without industries. You can talk about a world where people live with technology, or a world where we throw out all our technology. Just explain to us what kind of future you want to see.

When Ende finished speaking, the response was unexpected: five minutes of total silence.

He looked expectantly at the room, and they stared back. The pause became uncomfortable. You could hear a pin drop. Finally someone stood up and attacked him for asking the question. "What on earth was all that supposed to mean?" the manager complained. "What a bunch of nonsense! The objective fact is that if we don't continue 3 percent GDP growth, we are all doomed to economic ruin!"

"Please, haven't you been talking about that all day?" pleaded Ende. "Surely you can make room for talking about the big picture for just an hour?" But the attacks grew louder and harsher, and the moderator was forced to end the discussion.[10]

Why the silence and anger? Perhaps it was an acknowledgement that ideas about the future should be limited to fiction, where everyone will understand that they are fantasy and not to be taken seriously. Giving economists, who are devoted to quantifying human interests as a *scientific* pursuit, an inquiry into their own qualitative values is violating the sacred space of the scientific realm. The modern study of history faces the same problem.

An Inquiry into Values

Historians and archaeologists can verify material conditions and judge matters of authenticity with reasonable accuracy. But when we speak of the meaning of history, those who pretend to be objective researchers can no longer speak safely on the matter. No archaeologist will ever announce that she discovered the remains of a good king, or that new texts have been unearthed from an evil culture. These are "mere opinions," and outside the duty of scientists and historians to establish the facts. Yet it is not by facts alone, but through the force of our collective opinions, that we wreak our havoc on the world.

In recent years historians have found themselves limited to "objective" questions of cause and effect, so they have embraced a trendy "critical" paradigm that focuses on situating a person or a text as a product of local circumstances and context. Too many of the skeptical analyses of parahistory treat the content of these texts as almost irrelevant. To allow context to define meaning is to erase the intellect from the past and ignore the human desire not just to solve an immediate problem at hand, but aligns both the problem and the solution with higher principles, or laws, by which all problems can be understood. Only in this close reading of *content* can we find the answer to our question.

Of course, the possibility that anything can exist outside of history is a testy one these days. In modernity, per Julius Evola, "everything is believed to be conditioned and shaped by the age and by the times."[11] Moderns believe that their destiny is shaped, not by the power of heaven, but by forces called "historical inevitabilities," which carry us away from certain kinds of thinking that "belong" in the past, "inevitabilities" that demand a more "appropriate" accompaniment to the inexorable march of progress. The opinions of past ages on the worldview that triumphs today are apparently not worth thinking about.

What is most important in modernity is not understanding the end goal of the project but ensuring that human beings will serve as agents for its continued growth. Some moderns even believe *themselves* to be mere agents conditioned by circumstances to execute the will of "history," or even believe that they are animals with no soul, that all language is babble, and that people's attempts to impose order on the world are caused simply by historically outdated delusions. Believers will say that "it is an act of faith to assert that our thoughts have any relation to reality at all" (Chesterton), but moderns tell us that our only choice is to lose this faith, for "the people must be compelled to freedom" (Rousseau) and "we are condemned to be free" (Sartre).

People who believe in certain metaphysical principles, those that give humanity something immaterial to face toward, are accused by moderns of trying to "drag us backward" and out of our freedom, although what lies ahead is not well understood, and these days we do not always see the future as a cornucopia that giveth forth rivers of Coca-Cola and McDonald's to everyone forever. Despite this uncertainty, their insistence on the future continues to define their attitude toward the past. Our heritage is not seen as a record of kings, saints, gods, and heroes, healthy roots out of which a tree of virtue and strength may blossom, but is instead taken apart and "problematized" to uproot existing trees and ensure that no "delusions" interfere with the work of liberation and equalization.

This "problematization" has only frantically increased as belief in the future has faltered, thanks to an unspoken atmosphere in many universities and other public spaces that rewards those who offer such "deconstructions." Unconsciously they seem to worry that historical progress is not marching on as fast as it is supposed to and needs a little nudge to be hurried up the hill so that all might be condemned to freedom. When this mission is noticed and questioned, though, I have seen tenured professors grow downright nervous.

Currently it remains in official favor to believe that the historical laws that brought us to our current extravagance will continue to carry us onward and upward. In the near future, though, faith in secular, historical Providence will falter. There are two options from that point. One is to adopt a life-denying fatalism that regards civilization as a failed experiment on its way to its historically inevitable doom, and indeed we are aware of some who have adopted this attitude already. This is ludicrous and it will not be discussed any further. The other option is to turn toward tradition, toward a knowledge of a good and evil that is permanent and bound to neither time nor space.

The word *tradition* does not refer to the anachronistic preservation of irrelevant or harmful relics of the past in the present, nor has it ever meant this. Poor understanding of the concept by its representatives or opponents must not be confused with the meaning of the concept itself. When people speak reverently about the tradition of their ancestors they are referring to principles, positive in their teachings but opposed to modernity, which their ancestors executed in part. The *completeness* of Tradition, however, is not to be found in any human age, but lies in a realm that *exists in all ages*, even if it is not easily accessible. There is a beautiful tradition, if we allow ourselves to believe that Beauty exists. There is a truthful tradition, too, if we allow that Truth exists. The past can help edify us about these things if we have an eye for them. We will now briefly consider parahistory as seen through these eyes.

Memories of Truth

Acceptance of these parahistories inevitably relies upon an understanding that the ancients had a knowledge that has now been lost, but which through some effort can be remembered. In this book we have made extensive mention of the work of René Guénon and Julius Evola. Both writers considered such remembering possible, and considered all states and societies of premodern eras to have made extensive attempts to realize that memory of Tradition. The ancient Greeks, in fact, had a word for this process: *anamnesis*. As Socrates says in his dialogue with Meno:

> The soul, then, as being immortal, and having been born again many times, and having seen all things that exist, whether in this world or in the world below, has knowledge of them all; and it is no wonder that she should be able to call to remembrance all that she ever knew about virtue, and about everything; for as all nature is akin, and the soul has learned all things; there is no difficulty in her eliciting or as men say learning, out of a single recollection all the rest, if a man is strenuous and does not faint; for all enquiry and all learning is but recollection.

Why, then, is parahistory produced? We propose that it is because knowing Tradition is a process of *remembering,* and history is a means to *awaken memory.* Tradition is not a historical matter; billions of traditions are being carried on in the present day. But carrying on a tradition requires remembering it. This is where the act of writing history comes in, for "the truth of a history is grounded in the truth of the philosophy implemented by the historian."[12] In our particular case, when the official traditions become so inexplicable or irrelevant that readers fail to understand their truthful basis, an opening arises for parahistory. As Narasaki said, the *Nihon Shoki*, the *Kojiki*, and the parahistories are all attempts to interpret a single idea.

This suggests that parahistories are not really ultra-ancient. Of course, history and archaeology sometimes surprise us and upset the establishment. We now know that Homer's Trojan War really happened thanks to the work of amateurs who passionately believed in the Iliad. In Japan, a shopkeeper named Tadahiro Aizawa, working alone on abandoned sites out of a dogged love for ancient Japan, discovered the first Japanese Paleolithic artifacts in 1946, despite the scholarly consensus that Japan was uninhabitable in the Paleolithic era. The first fossils from the Edicarian period (600 million years ago) were identified in 1872, but the scientific establishment suppressed them until 1957. There may yet be surprises waiting for us beneath the ground in Japan or other places in the world. But these lovely counter examples cannot distract us from remembering that principles, not facticity, determine the worth of parahistory.

As stated in the introduction parahistory is a "romance in a fog," so a skeptical mind need not be forced to accept them as central to our view of history. The Catholic Church knew how to treat these documents of questionable authenticity: the category of *apocrypha*. Apocrypha are questionable, but are still included in the Catholic Bible as a source of wisdom to be taken with a grain of salt. Parahistories could be termed *historical apocrypha,* but unfortunately outside biblical studies the term "apocryphal" has taken on a completely negative connotation. Parahistory, in contrast, presents a positive order based in at least partially truthful principles.

The Parahistorical Order

The four texts I have discussed are completely different from each other in countless ways, but there is one thing that they share in common: they all remember the existence of an ultra-ancient state, which contained no self-contradictions, but had a unity of purpose expressed in art, science, and behavior alike. In other words, four very different memories of Japanese history have all presented us with an image of what Julius Evola calls an "organic State."

"The main thing that emerges in ancient forms," writes Evola, "is that unity in them did not possess a merely political character, but rather a spiritual and quite often religious one, the political domain apparently being shaped and upheld by an idea or a general view that was also articulated in thought, law, art, customs, cult, and the form of the economy. A unitary spirit was manifested in a choral variety of forms, corresponding to the various possibilities of human existence; in this context, *organic* and *traditional* are more or less synonymous terms."[13]

Indeed, parahistory is frequently trying to reconstruct this "unitary spirit." All of the texts unite Japan under a single Emperor and teaching, and two of them—the *Kujiki*-72 and Takenouchi Documents—try to prove through their ancientness that competing traditions should be united. If we look to Western parahistories we find that many of them are also trying to create the same kind of harmony in the same way. For example, the Lead Books of Sacromonte and the Gospel of Barnabas (see appendix B) present a synthesis of Christianity with Islam.

There is one important area in which our findings depart from Evola's expectations. Evola considered the truly organic State to be controlled by a *Männerbund* of supermen who conquer and subdue. They exercise prudence and contemplation, but only when they want to, for they are self-sufficient and take the lunar, feminine principle by force. The parahistories we have discussed do not reflect this. What is relayed to us in these documents is an ultra-ancient harmony of solar and lunar, an alchemical marriage that pursues balance, reflects higher unions in lower unions, and thereby causes people to rely on each other in strong but peaceful association. This is explicitly stated in the *Hotsuma Tsutaye* and Katakamuna Documents and implied in various places in the other documents as well.

Here we may understand why Guénon broke with Evola, who displayed a Nietzschean will to solar power and found ample backing for it in a revisionist history that portrayed Christianity as a "problematic influence" that undermines the power of the State.[14] In Guénon, on the other hand, we find a *synthesis* in the primordial state created by merging the left-hand path of Rigor and Justice with the right-hand path of Mercy and Peace. Christendom, which attempted to infuse the Justice of the pagan State with the Peace of the Mother Church, is a truthful tradition in Guénon's writings.[15] But I will not attempt here to assert the superiority of one writer to the other. For all their disagreement both writers display a stronger grasp of the ultra-ancient past than any before or since.

WELCOME HOME

At least tentatively, then, parahistory points to the existence of Tradition being recalled by its authors. Where does that leave those of us who are entranced by its visions of the past, but stuck in a very different modernity? Where are we to go from here? We might despair, and feel that we are being pulled backward in time, but it is time, in fact, which we are only beginning to understand. Our lives are not like a filmstrip or arrow pointing forward. Rather, we are bound to our friends and families by so many countless moments in the past, and by constantly running into the future we weaken our bonds with those around us.

Michael Ende, whom I mentioned earlier, also wrote a curious tale called *Momo,* which has become a fixture in schools in Korea and Germany. Momo, a girl who is very good at quietly listening and observing, discovers the existence of a group of "grey gentlemen" who are invisible unless you look very closely. These grey gentlemen are tricking people into viewing their life as a race against the clock, using a confusing show of facts and figures to "prove" how much time people are wasting by moving slowly through their little lives and being considerate. Under a sudden compulsion for time saving, people are forgetting what makes their lives worth living, and are working faster and faster to "make up for lost time"—but the time they think they are saving is all being consumed by the grey gentlemen, who do not allow anyone to learn of their presence. Momo is given the impossible task of finding a weakness in their system.

When Evola refers to an "insane restlessness" in modernity, a "non-stop race," "being bitten by a tarantula," this is precisely the behavior he is trying to describe. And like Evola, Ende saw this restlessness as having its origins in modernity. According to Ende early modern Europe created a myth of an "objective truth," which was opposed to "subjective opinions, rendered synonymous with illusion." This Newtonian science, which he contrasted with Goethean science, has successfully produced new technologies and revolutionized how we live our lives. But its so-called "objective, scientific truth" is only expressable through quantities—it has no conception of quality, and therefore cannot conceive of values. It can't tell us how to spend our time, only how to save it.[16]

Since they have no values themselves, the grey gentlemen fool people with quantities and figures. The only trick up their sleeve, in Ende's words, can be reduced to the claim that "everything has the same value, that is to say, everything is valueless." But anyone who actually believes such nonsense will come to feel that life itself is valueless. The grey gentlemen therefore encourage a false antimorality, pushing their blinded disciples to denounce the value judgments of the traditional, qualitative sphere, and embrace as its substitute a thoughtless race for bigger and faster quantities, "pressing toward an uncertain future, a crooked utopia." In their future every individual will be treated as if they were the same person, and the GDP will always get larger and larger.[17]

In truth, of course, nothing in this world is infinite. The quantity of our lives is limited by our deaths, and the quantity of oil on Earth is limited by the number of dead dinosaurs and fish we can suck out of the ground. This gives the lie to the race of the modern world, which never sees the end coming and can perceive of it only as failure. In the Traditional world the end is understood, accepted, and contemplated: something we never seem to have time for these days.

I will try not to spoil the end of *Momo,* which is worth reading, but obviously Ende believes the grey gentlemen can be defeated. When, at that moment of defeat, the urbanites suddenly feel that the need to rush and hurry has vanished from their souls, readers are given a glimmer of hope that our language of crisis and impending doom is unnecessary. Guénon's "crisis of the modern world" means only that modernity's unfulfillable promise of limitless quantities faces greater and greater crises. The world itself is not in danger. We are not in danger, either, if we can learn how to quit the race. In the words of John Michael Greer, "Collapse now, and avoid the rush!" Return to Tradition, and your crisis will be ended. It sounds easy enough, but unfortunately, it's not that easy in practice.

Ende once heard someone say that "World War III has already begun, but it is not being fought over land, but over time. We are already killing our own grandchildren." Modernity demands we do our part to consume and destroy the environmental and cultural resources of our own past and future. It is not so easy to switch sides in this ongoing war. We feel like a traitor to our prior convictions and are not sure where to find refuge. We feel anxious that we are not choosing the right side.

Because of the great confusion that the "grey gentlemen" have created all over the world, we have often been cut off from the life patterns of our ancestors, or, even if we have come to a book knowledge of a traditional group through careful research, we feel spiritually dislocated from them when we try to enter a living community, and we may find errors in their conception of Tradition as a disinterested outsider. It becomes necessary at this late stage of modernity to reveal many paths back to Tradition so that those who are outside and alone might at least find a vehicle they wish to board and that might be willing to bear them.

I hope this little book has been of some assistance in that regard. Each parahistorical window into the Traditional world has conveyed a possible path to be followed. Of course these documents do not explain the way for modern individuals to follow these paths, but they transcend the categories of religion, politics, myth, and history, and may confuse the "grey gentlemen" who have long been trying to subvert our understanding of all of these things. Perhaps a few stray souls might hear the songs of ultra-ancient Japan and stray from the march of Progress to be welcomed with open arms back to Tradition, as a child who remembers his parents might stray from the Pied Piper and return to Hamelin. It may be a long journey indeed, but at its end the traveler will hear the raucous greeting: "Welcome home!" Or, perhaps, *Okaeri nasai!*

We study history, it might be said, to learn who we are. We study parahistory, then, to discover who we *could be*. It upsets the view of history as a science of facts and delivers it into the realm of possibilities.

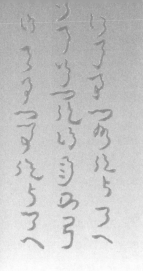

APPENDIX A

Time Line of
Japanese Parahistories

The following parahistories of Japan, complete to the best of my knowledge, are listed by the date each was reproduced in print and made available to other people—although often their stories do not begin with that printing.

936: *Sendai Kuji Hongi*
See chapter 2.

1670–1720: *Sendai Kuji Hongi Taiseikyō (various editions)*
See chapter 2.

1730: *Ancient Record of the Wakabayashi*
In 1730 a Toyama prefecture historian named Densuke Nozaki published a book entitled *Kankan-Sendatsu Roku* discussing many contemporary matters and recent history, but also claiming to convey some legends of Toyama prefecture from the eighth century, using a source called *Wakabayashi-ke Koki.* These Wakabayashi family records contain a large number of individuals who do not appear in the *Kojiki* or *Nihon Shoki,* including a female ruler named Anekurahime who defeated another matriarch and united the region, as in the Yamatai/ Himiko story, and then invented tools for weaving.[1] Although the

name Anekurahime can be found at a shrine in Toyama prefecture, the source Nozaki used cannot be found today, so these tales are considered parahistorical.

1764–1777: Hotsuma Tsutaye, Mikasafumi, Futomani
See chapter 3.

1873: Utsukushi-no-Mori Jinji

In the second year of the Meiji era the shrinekeeper of Ōmika Shrine found a record of the history of his shrine written in kamiyo moji. It is a twenty-page short story about "Yamatotake" (interestingly, the *Hotsuma Tsutaye*'s appelation for Yamatotakeru) and the shrine's provenance written in Ahiru grass-script, which had only recently been chosen by Atsutane Hirata as the kamiyo moji of choice. The fact that the text, written in kamiyo moji, describes events as recent as the Middle Ages is a little bewildering; Minoru Harada believes that the shrinekeeper might not have actually intended to make a claim of historicity.[2]

1873: The Uetsufumi

Sometime around 1820 Yoshizō Munakata, the headman of a tiny rural hamlet who produced no writings of his own and was probably illiterate, set out on foot to the regional capital with a manuscript passed down in his family for many generations. A scholar visiting from Kyoto examined the manuscript, saw that it was partially written in kamiyo moji, and dismissed it at once, since all such texts were considered forgeries. If he had been able to read it, though, he would have discovered that Emperor Jimmu was not the first Emperor of Japan, and in fact long before him, Japan had been the center of a great ultra-ancient civilization.

Munakata died in 1831 believing his "forgery" to be useless scrap paper. Luckily, when his wife gave it to local scholar Haesaka Sakimatsu for disposal, he soon realized it was of immense value and immediately began working on a translation of it, which he distributed to his colleagues. While the original was lost in a fire in 1873, in that same year an additional copy of the manuscript was discovered in the archives of the prestigious Ōtomo family.[3] This copy, which is mostly the same text but often uses different Chinese characters, is now in the Oita Prefectural Library, and in 2006 was designated a cultural asset of Usuki City, Oita. Shortly after these discoveries word of the manuscript, called *Uetsufumi,* came to Tokyo and some of the biggest names in the country began translating and commentating on it.

In 1877 a philologist named Yoshikaze Kira published an abridged translation of the *Uetsufumi* and a lengthy dissertation on its authenticity, which caused enough of a stir to be mentioned in European and American reports about Japan. Kira, as the humbled French commentator Léon de Rosny was forced to admit, was well studied in Japanese history and had found circumstantial evidence supporting the *Uetsufumi* in many rare books from the Edo period and earlier. In contrast Basil Hall Chamberlain, translator of the *Kojiki* and notable foreign speechmaker in Imperial Japan, opposed the authenticity of the *Uetsufumi* in his article "On Two Questions of Japanese Archaeology." In Japan, too, the government failed to take up the subject, and eventually interest died down.

Chamberlain was able to point out many absurd looking anachronisms in the *Uetsufumi.* The ancient civilization it describes possessed technology and customs that were not brought to the modern civilization of Japan until the 600s CE, such as paper, ink, royal headdress, and the imperial carriage. As is always the case for skeptics, Chamberlain limits himself to discussing what can be proven or disproven and does not discuss the higher value of the text at all.

Furthermore, if this a forgery, who forged it?! The Ōtomo manuscript and Munakata manuscript both appear to be copies of something that dates to far before the nineteenth century. It is strange indeed that the text only exists in two neglected copies, neither of which could have been forged by the people who discovered it. It claims to be the work of a thirteenth-century regent summarizing much older manuscripts he had come across, describing an ancient civilization based in Japan with a writing system of its own, and generally constitutes an encyclopedia of this hitherto unknown ancient world covering culture, customs, weights and measures, geography, language, calendar, astronomy, education, medicine, and exploration of foreign lands. It seems entirely possible that it may have really been written in the thirteenth century.

An Oita prefecture novelist and movie theater manager named Kan Misumi (1903–1971) claimed that these characters were actually the secret writing of the *sanka,* a word for nomads living in the Japanese mountains through the beginning of the Showa period. According to Misumi the sanka were forbidden by their elders to tell anyone about their secret writing system on penalty of death, and the author of the *Uetsufumi* killed thousands of sanka to steal their secrets and legends. However, this story is Misumi's alone. Although sanka was indeed a real word for mountain dwellers, it seems possible that Misumi invented the idea of a separate nomadic tribe within Japan himself because his claims have proven irreproducible, and the *Uetsufumi* claim especially is outlandish.

The *Uetsufumi* deserves further study from parahistorians. It claims an immense age for the Japanese nation, and makes a list of seventy-two emperors who ruled Japan before Jimmu, the last being Ugayafukiaezu, who is recorded in the *Nihon Shoki* and *Kojiki* as the father of Jimmu. Thus, the *Uetsufumi* is a mysterious, unresolved piece of evidence that attests to the Ugayafukiaezu dynasty of the Takenouchi Documents.

1886: New theory on the Ryukyu script

The *Ryukyu Shintōki,* a book of Buddhist divination, was written in the Ryukyu Islands in 1605. On one of its pages the author copied out a divination script in active use in the Ryukyus at that time. In 1886 an article appeared in the Tokyo Journal of Anthropology claiming that this was an ancient Okinawan script, and thus it now occupies a minor place in the world of parahistory.

1905: Khitan Legend

Kan'yū Hamana (1864–1938), a military official, published some texts he found during the Russo-Japanese War under the name *Kittan Koden,* documenting the descent of Susanowo to Korea's sacred mountain

Baekdu-san. The document apparently claims that Japanese, Koreans, and Manchus share common origins at Bek-sahn and in kingdoms along the Korean peninsula.

The title "Khitan Legend" belies the biggest challenge for researchers: proper nouns are written in the obscure, extinct Khitan language, which makes them difficult to identify with any Korean or Japanese equivalents.

1908: Tajima Prefect Documents

There is an oblique sentence from the *Kojiki* that says that a prince went to Tajima and defeated someone named Kugamimi-no-Mikasa whose real identity is forgotten. The Tajima Prefect documents, which are said to have been compiled by the prefects of Tajima Province over the years 814–974, claim that Mikasa was the leader of a band of powerful shamanesses and that the imperial warriors pursued Mikasa out to sea and were rescued from a storm by the gods of the sea. The documents were debunked by a historian in 1922 who explained that they were forged in 1810. The parahistorian Kiyohiko Agō, however, believed that they really were from the Heian period and thought they produced interesting parallels to the Takenouchi Documents.[4] There is something rather odd about the Takenouchi Documents having a reverse echo in a parahistory from 1810, but I don't know anything more about this. Agō's book is very rare and I have not yet seen a copy for myself.

1919: Report on the Ruins of Kai

The official histories and *Kujiki*-10 report that the province of Kai in modern Yamanashi prefecture was founded in the sixth century BCE, but that despite this prestigious history one of its leaders attempted to assassinate Emperor Suinin. A strange story indeed. Ujū Suda, a historian living in that area, spent years puzzling over a large collection of documents he found written from 712 to 1544 CE which contradict this story, and died before he could finish editing them. After his death in 1919 his son published his notes as the *Report on the Ruins of Kai* (*Kai Koseki Kō*).

This document claims that Kai was in fact one of the oldest and most loyal tribes in Japan, and demonstrates hidden meanings behind the names of old shrines in Yamanashi prefecture. Historical research suggests that the original kami of these shrines was in fact a *kui* 夔—a one-legged, mythical creature of ancient Chinese mythology that appears in the earliest Chinese writings 3000 years ago.[5]

1921–1945: Takenouchi Documents
See chapter 4.

1922: Miyashita, or Fuji Documents
The Miyashita Documents are a fragmentary text also known as the "Fuji Documents" since they claim that the most ancient Japanese civilization was centered at Mount Fuji rather than in the Nara area as is commonly accepted. They are also called the Jinnōki, the "Legends of the Kami Emperors," since they claim that Japan was settled by a Central Asian tribe who started a Takamagahara dynasty on Mount Fuji, and that Amaterasu, Tsukiyomi, and Susanowo were not gods but rulers of this ancient dynasty, which ended with Emperor Jimmu. Here, Mount Fuji is identified with the Mount Penglai of Chinese legend, and it is said that a court functionary named Xu Fu sailed there to find the elixir of immortality.

These documents, purported to be the only texts rescued from the Miyashita house after a fire in 1668, are recorded to have been the subject of a family dispute in 1863 when a Miyashita elder stole them during a funeral and ran off with them, destroying parts of the collection. The extant documents were published in 1922 and have names like the *Fujishi* and *Shina-Shintan Kōdaireki*.

The Miyashita Documents are sure to provide interesting research for parahistorians because some of what they say is attested in ancient Chinese sources that describe contemporary Japan as an exotic land full of wizards. Chinese histories tell us that Mount Fuji was indeed Mount Penglai, and Xu Fu really did sail there, and that there is an elixir there. Parallels have been drawn between the Miyashita Documents and the

Uetsufumi as well as the Indian epic Ramayana. For some reason they never achieved the fame of the Takenouchi Documents.[6]

1922: Nan'ensho

A quote from Thomas Havens' *Farm and Nation in Modern Japan* (1974) will here suffice. I have had to correct some inaccurate romanizations.

> [Minabuchi no] Shōan was a seventh-century Confucianist and tutor of the Tenji Emperor (r. 668–671) whose many writings had entirely disappeared by modern times, according to most scholars in [Seikyō] Gondō's day. Nan'ensho, its editors asserted, was based on a manuscript by [Minabuchi] himself that had belonged to the Gondō family for generations, supplemented by a variant text recently discovered in Sendai. The publishers of this work, composed in classical Chinese, were sufficiently satisfied of its authenticity to advertise that *Nan'ensho* was sixty years older than the *Kojiki* . . .
>
> Nan'ensho purported to be a record of questions and answers between [Minabuchi] and Tenji when the latter was crown prince. It described early invasions of Korea under [Emperor Jimmu], ancient Korean-Japanese trade contracts, victories and defeats in battle, and a harmonious rural society in ancient Japan governed by cooperation and mutual aid. Although the book was said to have been written at the height of Chinese cultural influence on Japan in the seventh century, its view of the state appeared to be closer to the utopian self-rule teachings of the Chinese philosophers Mencius and [Mozi] than to the imperial Confucianism patronized in Japan at the time.
>
> In the case of Nan'ensho, the public at large soon also became aware of its publication because Gondō and Ozawa dedicated the edition to [Emperor Meiji] and arranged for its formal presentation to the throne through the intervention of Prince Ichijō Saneteru. The newspapers immediately debated its authenticity without reaching a consensus . . .[7]

Gondō actually published what he called a translation of the Nan'ensho. Like the *Khitan Record* this parahistory claims that Susanowo was the forefather of Japan, Korea, China, and Manchuria. Also, like the Khitan Record it has found relatively little favor in modern times but was widely discussed in the imperial era. Minoru Harada believes that it may have had an impact on military officers who attempted an anti-modernist coup d'etat in February 1933.[8]

1939: Kuki Documents

In the Anglosphere there is a fairly popular school of karate called Kuki Shinden-ryū that claims to have been founded in the fourteenth century CE. However, there is no record of this school from before 1939 when a man named Ichiro Miura announced that he had been granted exclusive access to the Kuki family archives. The documents he found are called the Kuki Documents and attest to the ancient provenance of the karate school, among other things.

Anyone who has visited a Japanese elementary school has doubtless seen a statue of the child prodigy Kinjirō Ninomiya (1787–1856), usually in the front courtyard. Ninomiya, a lifelong reader and Buddhist economist, owned a large library in adulthood, and in 1843 he offered some Kuki Shinto texts to a friend. This is the first known reference to unique "Kuki documents," but proponents of these documents do not usually mention Ninomiya's rather harsh evaluation of them: "It would be no loss for me to part with them," he writes. There is no evidence that the texts Ninomiya held have any relation to the 1939 documents.[9] Some proponents of these documents hold that they were seized from Izawa-no-miya in the 1600s (see chapter 2), but there is no evidence for this. On the other hand, there is strong evidence that Miura was involved in new religious groups.

In Miura's transcription of the Kuki text, *Amatsu-Tatara Hifumi,* there are many passages that resemble the Takenouchi Documents including the Five-Colored Races, the appearance of Jesus, Moses, Buddha, and Noah, and the visits of the Emperors to Egypt and other countries. It also explicitly shares the claim of the *Uetsufumi* and

Takenouchi Documents that there was an Emperor Ugayafukiaezu who was the "73rd of his dynasty." It is apparent that the Kuki Documents are derived from the Takenouchi Documents, which appeared twenty years earlier. There are some who say that Miura was modifying real Kuki documents, but the existence of real Kuki documents outside of Miura's description has yet to be confirmed. The parahistorian Kiyohiko Agō, who also believed in the Takenouchi Documents, wrote a postwar book about the Kuki Documents where he referred to them as the "Kukami Documents." The only source for this pronunciation is Agō; since they allegedly belonged to the Kuki family, I call them the Kuki Documents.

The Kuki Documents claim to be written by descendants of the Izumo kingdom and criticize Prince Shōtoku, the famous promoter of Buddhism, claiming that he murdered Emperor Sushun and was a hoaxer posing as a crown prince. The parahistorical section of the documents, though, is subsidiary to the utility they have to the Kuki household, which produced and currently owns these documents, namely to justify the claim that they transmit a most ancient and powerful style of martial arts. Barring any evidence I have overlooked here, this claim appears to have begun with that 1939 discovery.

1941: Secret History of the Akita Mononobe

The Mononobe clan are tied up with the authorship of the *Sendai Kuji Hongi* (*Kujiki*-10), but the Akita branch of that clan has long preserved some secret histories, which are not found in any printed document, written partially in a kamiyo moji called Ahiru Grass Script. The documents have some similarities with the *Kujiki*-10, such as a tradition of Ten Imperial Treasures instead of three, a similar list of early kami, and a mention of the Ame-no-Iwafune, here called Ame-no-Torifune. The most notable difference is that the kami descend to Earth in Tohoku rather than elsewhere in Japan.[10]

As of yet nobody has undertaken a serious investigation of this matter, except for parahistorians who happily fold the text into their existing world of secret histories from Tohoku. One writer has commented that these books are so undramatic that it seems they might not be parahistory at all, but a real minor history that has been improperly marginalized with the most recent manuscript of the documents dating to 1711, although not published until 1941.[11]

1948: Ekidan Shiryō

A writer named Shiichi Kubota (1913–1984) began referencing two books called *Kataiguchiki* and *Itanki* for his historical claims in 1948. He said these books came from his household but never made them public or even quoted directly from them, which makes his claims somewhat suspicious.

1966: Katakamuna Documents

See chapter 5.

1973: Shinden Jōdai Tennōki

Kiyohiko Agō (1909–2003) spent many years documenting Japan's parahistories and uncovering many obscure documents. While he made waves in the small occult world, his research publications are quite rare. One of his finds, the *Shinden Jōdai Tennōki,* was buried in the pages of an obscure Shinto journal in 1973 and has not been looked at since. This document attests to the Ugayafukiaezu dynasty found in the *Uetsufumi.* Agō says it was found in a used bookstore in Fukuoka in 1882, which would have been at the height of the *Uetsufumi* boom, and direct quotes from the 1877 commentary on the *Uetsufumi* were inscribed in the margins, so it seems that someone was trying to collaborate the two manuscripts.[12]

1976: Tsugaru Soto Sangunshi

Tsugaru Soto Sangunshi is an interesting example of a parahistory that became a standard history for some years in postwar Japan. It claims to date to the Middle Ages, but contains references to the continent of Mu and modern terms like quasar, light year, and Pluto. Despite this, its antiauthority depiction of a pre-Japanese kingdom in Tohoku was intriguing enough that it was continuously cited on Japanese television in the 1980s and 1990s, and some academics such as Professor Takehiko Furuta continue to propound its veracity. Actually, even the sympathetic scholar Akira Fujiwara has concluded that it could not have been written at any point before 1976.[13]

The author, Kihachirō Wada, claimed to have discovered these texts in the records of the Wada family. The text, written partially in kamiyo moji, describes a tribe called Arahagaki that had its own kingdom in Tohoku, which the text describes as "Mongoloid" and which was brutally conquered by the Yamatai tribe of Himiko, who the text describes as "Aryan." Professor Furuta, lately of Tohoku University, has used this as a basis for books like *"Kimigayo" Praises Kyushu: A People's History* and *Stolen Myths,* which claim that the *Kojiki* and *Nihon Shoki* were written to oppress the histories of the Arahagaki and other tribes, that Yamatai never existed, and that the sitting Emperor is an impostor from Kyushu. His most major critic is the skeptic Minoru Harada, who discovered some of the obvious anachronisms I mention here.

1980: Saga of Jōkan Tomi of Izumo

The saga of the Izumo chief Jōkan Tomi is an oral parahistory related by writer Taiyō Yoshida in his book *The Mystery of the Izumo Empire.* This oral history was passed down secretly from generation to generation and tells the story of how the Izumo Empire was defeated by the upstart Yamato people. Mr. Yoshida has also graced us with a translation of the *Kojiki* and *Nihon Shoki* as they are meant to be read—in Sumerian!

1983: Kasuga Documents

The book *Ametsuchi no Kotofumi* in the Kuki Documents claims the true history was preserved by various families whose names were: Moriya, Takeuchi, Kasuga, and Ōnakatomishi. In 1983 Kiyohiko Agō wrote a book on the Kuki Documents that claimed the Takeuchi record was the Takenouchi Documents, Moriya was the Akita Mononobe Documents, Ōnakatomishi was another of the Kuki Documents, and the Kasuga record referred to documents held privately by the prewar parahistorian Kouon Kasuga, which attest to a common origin of Jews and Japanese. Nobody else seems to know anything about this, and Agō's private papers have gone missing since his death.

1992: Masumi Tantōshō

In 1992 the author Kazuha Ogura introduced a new parahistory called *Masumi Tantōshō* that elaborates on the story in the official histories of Prince Oke and Prince Woke, who murdered their father in 456 CE and became itinerant actors on the run, only to be hired by the imperial court twenty-five years later and reunited with their family. Ogura's "discovery" appears to be historical fiction, and his claim that he found a real manuscript of the text confuses his readers, but Minoru Harada does indicate that there is some mystery and ambiguity about the story as Ogura tells it.[14]

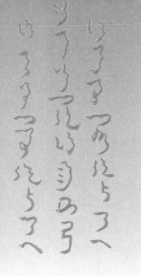

Time Line of Western Parahistories

There are countless books about non-Japanese parahistories, but very few summarize parahistory as a genre. This brief, incomplete appendix might be able to point readers in the right direction. It may prove enlightening to compare the chronology of these texts to some of the Japanese texts I have discussed.

1595: *Lead Books of Sacromonte*

In Sacromonte, Spain, a newly Christianized city seized from the Moors, a series of "lead books" appeared over the period 1595 to 1599, which explain that the descendants of the Moors in the city are actually the heirs of St. Cecilio, a medieval saint of rumor who founded an ancient Christian church in Spain. They also tell of secret messages from the Virgin Mary, who is planning a future release of a document called the *Certainty of the Gospel* that will unite all nations and religions. It describes Jesus as a prophet with amazing powers but as fully human and not the Son of God. Recently a good discussion of the history surrounding the books was released in English: A. Katie Harris, *From Muslim to Christian Grenada* (Baltimore, Md.: Johns Hopkins University Press, 2007). However this book does not discuss the content of the texts in depth.

1709: Gospel of Barnabas

The Gospel of Barnabas is a book of possibly Gnostic, possibly Arabic, possibly Italian origin. A single manuscript survives that dates to sometime before 1709. Like the Lead Books a century before, it describes Jesus as a prophet but not the Son of God, and says he was not crucified, but that Judas was crucified in his place. (Takenouchi reseachers take note!)

The text then continues to discuss early Christian history, calling Saint Paul "deceived," and says that Jesus never called himself the Messiah but rather said that a future prophet and Messiah would be coming named Mohammed. It would appear to be a Muslim forgery, but Jesus explicitly permits alcohol, requires circumcision, and forbids polygamy, which conflicts with Muslim teachings about Jesus's message. All in all, the work appears to have been produced in medieval Europe, astonishing enough considering its endorsement of some Muslim views.

1751: Book of Jasher

A "rediscovered" Gospel that was notably reprinted by the Rosicrucian Order in 1934. For this and other such biblical pseudepigraphia, see *Famous Biblical Hoaxes, or, Modern Apocrypha,* by Edgar J. Goodspeed (1931).

1760: Ossian Poems

In the late eighteenth century the Scottish poet James Macpherson claimed to have discovered a new cycle of epic Gaelic poems, set in a golden age. One critic, Reverend Hugh Blair, wrote that regardless of the factuality of Macpherson's "discovery" the poems of Ossian strike a deep chord, for in them "we find the fire and enthusiasm of the most early times, combined with an amazing, degree of regularity and art. We find tenderness, and even delicacy of sentiment, greatly predominant over fierceness and barbarity. Our hearts are melted with the softest feelings, and at the same time elevated with the highest ideas of magnanimity, generosity, and true heroism." A comparison to the *Hotsuma Tsutaye* seems apt. These poems became so popular that they inspired

Figure B.1. Ossian receiving the ghosts of the French heroes (1800).

much beautiful Renaissance art (figure B.1) and got appreciative reviews from Napoleon and Thomas Jefferson.

1830–1845: Book of Mormon and Voree Plates

The Book of Mormon's placement in this appendix could be questionable, since it is the official history of the Church of Jesus Christ of Latter Day Saints and some other large groups. Nor could I reasonably be asked to summarize what it is and why it is studied in this appendix. But it remains parahistorical with regard to American history at large. For more information, I recommend Paul C. Gutjahr's recent study *The Book of Mormon: A Biography* (Princeton University Press, 2012).

1867: Oera Linda Book

Like the *Uetsufumi,* the Oera Linda Book emerges from a murky and poorly documented history in the nineteenth century. In this case, the first firm fact we have about the document is that the amateur scholar Cornelis Over de Linden (1811–1874) attempted to donate it to a library in 1867; he failed, but soon found a large audience to appreciate his discovery in both the Netherlands and overseas.

Like many of the Japanese parahistories Oera Linda claims to be an ancient copy of an even more ancient original. Two letters appended to the beginning of the document are dated 803 and 1256 CE, and claim to be part of the household line secretly passing the document from father to son. These testimonies are perhaps only a natural addition to a document that claims to come from 2194 BCE. It would be more surprising if no reason were supplied for its secretive existence.

Like the Japanese parahistories the Oera Linda Book was written with a specific people in mind: the Frisians of the northern Netherlands, whom it claims were in ancient times an incredibly powerful race. The Frisians of 2194 BCE were a pagan civilization whose folk-mothers had ruled over most of Europe and some other continents as well for millions of years. The book draws heavily on mythology, identifying the Frisians with the Celtic goddess Frya/Freyja, and advises the modern Frisians to preserve their language and race.

Finally, like the Japanese parahistories, Oera Linda also has its own language and ancient writing system! (See figure B.2.) However it honestly makes the Japanese attempts look fairly creative—the writing system is not particularly imaginative, and the language used bears a closer resemblance to modern Dutch than Old Frisian.

This parahistory found an unlikely proponent in the German musicologist Herman Wirth, who had long nurtured a belief in pre-Roman civilization in northern Europe and published a lavish examination of the parahistory in 1928, the same year the Takenouchi Documents

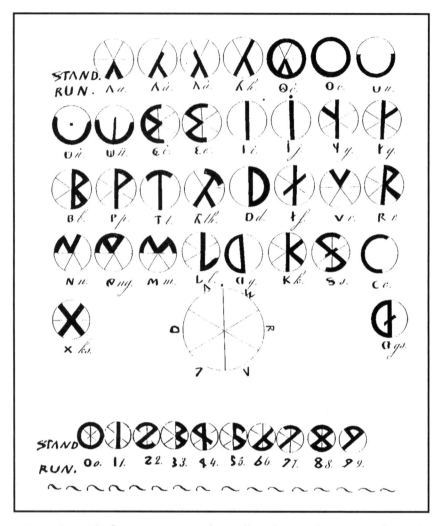

Figure B.2. The kamiyo moji, if I dare call it that, of the Oera Linda Book.

appeared in Japan. Wirth became a pariah for his beliefs and fell into intermittent poverty for the rest of his life, but his book was deeply inspiring to Julius Evola.

1888: Book of Dzyan

Similar to the Book of Mormon but less known is the Book of Dzyan, a Tibetan ultra-ancient history relayed by H. P. Blavatsky, founder of the Theosophical Society. Once again, this is neither the time nor place to summarize the teachings and history of Theosophy. Suffice to say Blavatsky knew the text she was producing was unknown to the West and that she risked ridicule for it, but she grouped it with the "books of Kiu-te," a term that was identified over eighty years later as the real Chinese word for the Buddhist Tantras. David Reigle's *Blavatsky's Secret Books* (Mecosta, Mich.: Wizards Bookshelf, 1999) is the seminal study of this difficult text.

1894: Life of Saint Issa

A poorly documented Russian Jewish spy (?) living in Paris named Nicolas Notovich (1858-?) claimed in an 1894 book to have been traveling through Tibet when he discovered a manuscript about Jesus in the monastery of Hemis, Ladakh, India. The document claims that Jesus, born in Israel, came to India to study the teaching of Buddha; that he learned Pali and the Vedas; and, finally, that he returned to Jerusalem and was put to death by Pontius Pilate. This otherwise rather interesting, if astounding, document is a bit ruined in my opinion by that final section, which suggests that someone traveled from Palestine to Tibet immediately after the Crucifixion and was somehow able to discover this remote monastery where Jesus had studied and return to Palestine to tell the monks about Jesus's final days. The existence of this document can be disproven or confirmed, depending on whom you ask, by visiting the monastery in Ladakh and asking to see it for yourself.

1967: Dossiers Secrets d'Henri Lobineau

See pages 154–55.

1968: Essene Gospels

The Hungarian Edmond Bordeaux Székely (1905–1979) is described on Wikipedia as a "philologist/linguist, philosopher, psychologist and natural living experimenter." He founded something called the International Biogenic Society to espouse scientific vegetarianism, and claimed in 1968 that he had discovered secret Gospels of the Essenes in the Vatican Library, which he subsequently published. He later founded the "new science" of Archeosophy, which attempts to reconstruct the Original Knowledge from sources so ancient we no longer even possess them. If all this sounds rather similar to the Katakamuna Documents, which appeared in the same year, I'm afraid I do not know what to say.

1977: Simon Necronomicon

I dare not describe the contents of this infernal book . . . the horror . . . *the horror!* For those whose capacity for madness is greater than mine, please consult Daniel Harms's and John Wisdom Gonce III's *The Necronomicon Files: The Truth Behind the Legend* (York Beach, Me.: Red Wheel/Weiser, 2003).

1984: Bock Saga

Ior Bock (1942–2010) was a Swedish-speaking Finnish mythologist who claimed at his mother's funeral in 1984 that she had left him the duty of releasing their family's secret mythological saga to the world. It covers such important matters as the origin of the Nordic peoples, of European monarchies, of pagan traditions, and some unique sexual practices of ancient times.

1994: The Kolbrin

The earliest sections of the Kolbrin were written, so it says, in 1600 BCE in Egypt in Hieratic script. These were brought to Britain by the Phoenicians, and in 100 CE the Celts contributed a section in Old Celtic. In 1184 these manuscripts were rescued from a burning Glastonbury Abbey and preserved by a secret society in Scotland. Somehow it then made its way to New Zealand, where a group called "The Culdian Celestial Age Trust" (a name that draws on an obscure medieval Celtic group called the Culdees) was entrusted with it, copyrighted it, and finally got around to publishing it in 1994 after 3,600 years. All information about the book comes from the Trust.

The book begins with an account of human creation that follows the Bible story but contradicts it. The Egyptians relate reports from an even more ancient source that spoke of dinosaurs, natural catastrophes, and plagues. They also discuss a civilization of unknowable age called the Ramakui whose emissary, called the Great One and the Chief Guardian of the Mysteries, instructed the Egyptians in writing, storytelling, agriculture, worship, building houses, and so forth. The Passover story is told from the perspective of the Egyptians, and the inner workings of the Druids are explained by the Celts. The early kings of Britain are listed, but differ from the standard historical list. In other words, a surprising wealth of revelations is provided about the origin of the Western world along with hints of information that precedes our earliest records.

Originally consisting of twenty-one books—twelve books written by the Celts about Britain, eight by the Egyptians, one by the Trojans—only eleven remain today. Many scrolls and volumes were destroyed over the centuries. But it's okay, because the printed book is also referred to as the "Open Book" or "Great Book of Life," with the other sections being the "Closed Book," which sounds like a book that is not supposed to be published. The medieval text was written in an otherwise unattested "old alphabet of thirty-six letters," which later became "biblical English," and in the early twentieth century the text was "modernized" again and now reads like contemporary English. It may be purchased from the Culdian Trust for about $100, or from a pirate publisher for about $50.

Notes

INTRODUCTION.
A ROMANCE IN A FOG

1. Evola, *Revolt,* 183.
2. Ibid., 3.
3. Imura, "Arafuka Michinari," 69.

CHAPTER I.
PASSPORT TO PARAHISTORY:
ANCIENT JAPAN'S MYSTERIES

1. Sakai, *Jindai Hishi Hyakuwa,* 2.
2. Evola, *Revolt,* 5.
3. Ibid., 42.
4. Aston, *Nihongi,* 1–3; and Philippi, *Kojiki,* 47.
5. Philippi, *Kojiki,* 71.
6. Ibid, 79.
7. Aston, *Nihongi,* 110–11, 128.
8. Ibid., 111–16, 134; and Philippi, *Kojiki,* 167–70.
9. Aston, *Nihongi,* 134; and Philippi, *Kojiki,* 181.
10. Aston, *Nihongi,* 176; and Philippi, *Kojiki,* 226.
11. Aston, *Nihongi,* 15, 83; and Philippi, *Kojiki,* 52, 82–83.

CHAPTER 2.
PRINCE SHŌTOKU'S LOST CLASSIC:
SENDAI KUJI HONGI TAISEIKYŌ

1. Hideki, "Sendai kuji," 2–13.
2. Aston, *Nihongi,* 432; and Teeuwen, "Sendai Kuji Hongi," 87–96.
3. Bentley, *Sendai Kuji Hongi;* and Teeuwen, "Sendai Kuji Hongi."
4. Kōno, *Kuji-Taiseikyō;* and Harada, "Mō Hitotsu," 360.
5. Chouon, *Shigetsu Yawa,* 155–56.
6. Iwada, "Kōtai Jingū," 46; and Torii, *Amaterasu Ōmikami,* 206–8.
7. Harada, "Mō Hitotsu," 357–59.
8. Norinaga, *Two Shrines of Ise,* 22n; and Bentley, *Sendai Kuji Hongi,* 14, 396n.
9. Gotō, T, *Sakitsumiyo no Furukoto,* 32.
10. Torii, *Nihon Chōkodaishi,* 82–83; and Nakaya, "Shōtoku Taishi"; and Ogasawara, *Zoku Shintō Taikei,* 108-13.
11. Nakaya, "Shōtoku Taishi"; and Miyatō, *Shōtoku Taishi ni Erabu,* 315.
12. Yoda, *Hen Mui Shinpi Shoden.*
13. Scheid, "Reading the *Yuiitsu,*" 117–43.
14. Nozawa, *Kinsho Shotōku,* 15.
15. Aston, *Nihongi,* 129–32.
16. Miyatō, *Shōtoku Taishi ni Erabu,* 25–66; Nozawa, *Kinsho,* 73–76.
17. Evola, *Ruins,* 155.
18. Ibid., 171ff.
19. Aston, *Nihongi,* 132.
20. Miyatō, *Shōtoku Taishi ni Erabu,* 257.
21. Ishida, *Shakugi,* 7.
22. Evola, *Ruins,* 162.
23. Miyatō, *Shōtoku Taishi ni Erabu,* 264; Nozawa, *Kinsho,* 128, 201; Ishida, *Shakugi,* unnumbered page in manuscript.
24. Bentley, *Sendai Kuji Hongi,* 155–56.
25. Ibid., 209; and Aston, *Nihongi,* 44, 373.
26. Shintō Taikei Hensankai, *Taiseikyō III,* 51.
27. Ibid., 52.

28. Harada, *Gensō no Kodai ōchō,* 194–98; and e-mail communication with Matt Treyvaud.

29. Yuasa, "Masuho Zankō," 315–23.

CHAPTER 3.
FINNEGAN'S WAKA:
THE *HOTSUMA TSUTAYE* AND WOSHITE CORPUS

1. Matsumoto, Legends, 59.

2. Ibid., 63.

3. Ibid., 58.

4. Ikeda, *Hotsuma Tsutaye,* 18.

5. Matsumoto, *Legends,* 35–36.

6. Matsumoto, �🔲 ✳ ⊕ ✳ ♉ ♠, 51; and Torii, *Nihon Chōkodaishi,* 87.

7. Matsumoto, �🔲 ✳ ⊕ ✳ ♉ ♠, 48–50.

8. Kanō, "Amatsukyō," 372.

9. Torii, *Nihon Chōkodaishi,* 101; and Kiyosuke, "'Hotsuma Tsutaye,'" 179.

10. Matsumoto, �🔲 ✳ ⊕ ✳ ♉ ♠, 37.

11. Matsumoto, *Legends,* 139.

12. Ibid., 37–41.

13. Torii, *Amaterasu,* 128.

14. Ikeda, *Hotsuma Tsutaye,* 154.

15. Torii, *Hotsuma Monogatari,* 36.

16. Fujiwara, *Nihon no Gisho,* 129; and Fujiwara, "Chūyo Nihongi,"159.

17. Evola, *Revolt,* 235.

18. Matsumoto, *Himerareta,* 61–67; and Matsumoto, *Legends,* 83–85.

19. Matsumoto, *Legends,* 77.

20. Ikeda, *Legends,* 7–8.

21. Matsumoto, *Legends,* 92–94.

22. Ibid., 86–88.

23. Ikeda, *Legends,* 29–30.

24. Torii, *Hotsuma Monogatari,* 188–89.

25. Torii, *Amaterasu,* 206–7.

26. Ibid., 111, 114.

27. Fujiwara, *Nihon no Gisho,* 130; and Fujiwara, "Chūyo Nihongi," 159.

28. Torii, *Amaterasu*, 102–9.

29. Ikeda, *Hotsuma Tsutaye*, 233.

30. Ikeda, *Legends,* 13–14; and Torii, *Amaterasu*, 186.

31. Ikeda, *Hotsuma Jōmon*, 70.

32. Evola, *Meditations,* 13.

33. Ooms, *Imperial Politics,* 234.

CHAPTER 4.
JAPANESE ATLANTIS, CHRIST, AND PYRAMIDS:
THE TAKENOUCHI DOCUMENTS

1. Evola, *Revolt,* 22.

2. Suzumu, "State Shinto," 61-61.

3. Morrow, "Patriotism," 2–29.

4. Kōsaka, *Takenouchi Documents I,* 350–428.

5. Evola, *Revolt,* 9.

6. Kōsaka, *Takenouchi Documents II,* 6.

7. Guénon, *King of the World,* 26.

8. Plato, *Critias* CXIII.

9. Kōsaka, *Takenouchi Documents II,* 38.

10. Guénon, *Traditional Forms,* 29.

11. Aston, *Nihongi,* 110, 128; and Okada, "Koshi-koden to UFO," 128.

12. Fuse, 'Takenouchi Monjo,' 70–72; 82–84.

13. Kōsaka, *Takenouchi Documents I,* 119.

14. Evola, *Revolt,* 8.

15. Kōsaka, *Takenouchi Documents II,* 217–18.

16. Guénon, *King of the World,* 72

17. Kōsaka, *Takenouchi Documents I,* 205.

18. Nakazono, *Source,* 59–64.

19. Fuse, 'Takenouchi Monjo' 2, 274–80.

20. Guénon, *King of the World,* 29.

21. Nakazono, *Source,* 59–64.

22. Kōsaka, *Takenouchi Documents I,* 388; and Kōsaka, *Takenouchi Documents II,* 276.

23. Guénon, *King of the World,* 52.

24. Kōsaka, *Chōzukai*, 261.

25. Kōsaka, *Takenouchi Documents I*, 293–97.

26. Ibid., 248–75.

27. Takeuchi, "Mou hitotsu no," 82–91; and Fuse, *Takenouchi Monjo no Nazo wo Toku 2*.

28. Kume, *Sakai Katsutoki*, 393.

29. Fuse, *Nazo wo Toku*, 33, 38.

30. Sakai, "The Three Elements of Music," 406.

31. Kume, *Sakai Katsutoki*, 239.

32. Ibid., 234, 241.

33. Evola, "Il barone sanguinario."

34. Sakai, *Sekai no Shōtai*, 300–301.

35. Kume, *Sakai Katsutoki*, 374–78.

36. Fuse, *Nazo wo Toku*, 234–38; Kume, *Sakai Katsutoki*, 426–27.

37. Evola, *Revolt*, 56.

38. Sakai, *Jindai Hishi Hyakuwa*, 256.

39. Ibid., 259.

40. Kume, *Sakai Katsutoki*, 268, 301.

41. Fuse, *Nazo wo Toku*, 100.

42. Sakai, *Jindai Hishi Hyakuwa*, 10, 19, 228.

43. Kume, *Sakai Katsutoki*, 620–30.

44. Ibid., 407.

45. Fuse, *Nazo wo Toku*, 28.

46. Tsushima, "Emperor," 491.

47. Kiku, *Kirisuto*, 220, 224.

48. Kōsaka, *Takenouchi Documents I*, Preface (unnumbered).

49. Nakazono, *Source*, 218–37.

50. Godwin, *Atlantis*, 279.

51. Cayce, *Mysteries*, 30.

52. Inoue, "Sano Tsunehiko."

53. "Ushinawareta," 64, 69; Harada, "Kisho," 170; and Churchward, *Books*.

54. Fuse, *Nazo wo Toku*, 280.

55. Kōsaka, *Takenouchi Documents II*, 104–9.

56. Maier, *Totalitarianism,* 205.

57. Fujiwara, *Nihon no Gisho.*

58. Tsushima, "Emperor."

59. Goodman, *Jews in the Japanese Mind,* 156–57.

60. Masaki, Diary of, 77, 136–37, 216, and Nagaki, "Kirisuto," 3.

61. Guénon, *King of the World,* 73–74.

62. Kōsaka, *Takenouchi Documents II,* 278–79.

CHAPTER 5.
ANCIENT SCIENCE FOR MODERN MYSTICS: THE KATAKAMUNA DOCUMENTS

1. Guénon, *Crisis,* 50.

2. Nakaya, quoted in Harada, *Tondemo,* 189.

3. Akiyoneto, *Nazo,* 41–42.

4. Harada, *Tondemo,* 187–88.

5. Gotō, Y, "Kekarechi."

6. Tadashii Kyōiku wo Mamoru Kai, *Nihon no Jōkodai Bunka,* 15; and Okumura, *Manshū Nyannyan Kō* referenced in Ofuka, "Manshū no Byōe," 66.

7. Akutsu, "Kagaku," 143.

8. Guénon, *Man,* 12.

9. *Sōjishō* XI and *Shinji,* Ki no Maki, as quoted on the blog http://teru. under.jp.

10. *Sōjishō* V, quoted in Akiyoneto, *Nazo,* 240.

11. Harada, *Tondemo,* 190.

12. *Sōjishō* X, quoted in Fukano, *Chōkagakusho,* 59–73.

13. Guénon, *King of the World,* 10.

14. *Sōjishō* III, quoted in Sekigawa, *Michi,* 31–32.

15. Fukano, *Chōkagakusho,* 55.

16. Guénon, *Reign of Quantity,* 137.

17. Akiyoneto, *Nazo,* 250.

18. Guénon, *Reign of Quantity,* 31.

19. Guénon, *King of the World,* 11.

20. Guénon, *Crisis,* 17.

21. McGilchrist, *Emissary*, 14.

22. Fukano, *Chōkagakusho*, 220–21.

23. Akiyoneto, *Nazo*, 93.

24. Sekigawa, *Michi*, 221, 244.

25. Ibid., 88.

26. Funai, *Iyashirochi;* and Sekigawa, *Michi*, 102–3.

27. Sekigawa, *Michi*, 151.

28. Ibid., 265.

29. Ibid., 88–89.

30. Guénon, *King of the World*, 50–51.

31. Harada, *Tondemo*, 188.

32. Fukano, *Chōkagakusho;* and Nagaike, *Senshō Energy*.

33. Michel, *Earth Spirit*.

CONCLUSION:
PARAHISTORY AND THE GREY GENTLEMEN

1. Fujiwara, "Kindai no Gisho," 201–2.

2. Ehrman, *Forged*, 120.

3. Barber, *Earth from Sky*, 120.

4. Tolkien, *Reader*, 24.

5. Plato, *Phaedrus*.

6. Nasr, "Reply," 635.

7. Isomae, *Sono Keifu*.

8. Morrow, "Patriotism," 2–29.

9. Fitzgerald, "Religion."

10. Ende et al., *Oriibu*, 38.

11. Evola, *Men*, 117.

12. Marrou, *De la connaissance*, 237.

13. Evola, *Men*, 149.

14. Ibid., 212–13.

15. Guénon, *King of the World*, 15–16.

16. Evola, *Men*, 172–73; Ende et al., *Oriibu*, 38.

17. Ende et al., *Oriibu*, 59.

APPENDIX A:
TIME LINE OF JAPANESE PARAHISTORIES

1. Harada, *Kamigami,* 165–67.
2. Ibid., 148–52.
3. Tanaka, K., *Gishokō.*
4. Harada, "Kojima *Kojiki*," 186–87.
5. Harada, *Kamigami,* 116–23.
6. Rekishi Dokuhon, "Koshi-Koden Catalog," 22–23.
7. Havens, *Farm,* 174–75.
8. Harada, *Kamigami,* 182–83.
9. Saitō, "'Kukami Bunken,'" 259–60.
10. Tanaka, S., "Mononobe Bunsho," 103–4.
11. Takahashi, "Mohaya Boku," 55.
12. Harada, "Koshi-koden Jiten," 386.
13. Fujiwara, "Kindai no Gisho," 217.
14. Harada, *Kamigami,* 152–58.

Glossary
of Japanese Terms

This is a glossary of Japanese and Chinese names found in the text. In this list Japanese names are listed with family name last, the way they were presented in the text of the book.

Akira Fujiwara　藤原明

Akiyoneto　阿基米得

Amaterasu　天照大神

Atsutane Hirata　平田篤胤

Běishān　北山

Dainihonshi　大日本史

Dogū　土偶

Dōkai Chouon　潮音道海

Ekidan Shiryō　易断史料

Gekū　外宮

Haesaka Sakimatsu　幸松葉枝

Himiko　卑弥呼

Hira Tōji　平十字

Hitsuki Shinji　日月神示

Inbe 忌部

Ise Jingū 伊勢神宮

Ittei Ishida 石田一鼎

Jilin 吉林

Jimmu 神武天皇

Jinnin 神人

Jinzaburō Masaki 真崎甚三郎

Jirō Sekigawa 関川二郎

Jōkan Tomi 富上官

Jōmon 縄文

Kai Koseki Kō 甲斐古蹟考

Kami 神

Kamiyo 神代

Kamiyo moji 神代文字

Kan Misumi 三角寛

Kanna Hifumi no Tsutae 神字日文傳

Kasuga 春日

Katsutoki Sakai 酒井勝軍

Kinjirō Ninomiya 二宮金次郎

Kittan Koden 契丹古伝

Kiyohiko Agō 吾郷清彦

Kiyomaro Takeuchi 竹内巨麿

Kofun 古墳

Kogo Shūi 古語拾遺

Kokoro 心

Kokugaku 国学

Kojiki 古事記

Ko-Shinto　古神道

Kōso Kōtai Jingū　皇祖皇太神宮

Kugamimi-no-Mikasa　陸耳御笠

Kujiki　旧事紀

Kuki　九鬼

Kuranosuke Kyōgoku　京極内蔵助

Lú Yōu Sān　蘆有三

Masafumi Kume　久米晶文

Masumi Tantōshō　真清探當證

Mikoto Nakazono　中薗雅尋

Minoru Harada　原田実

Mitogaku　水戸学

Mitsuru Ikeda　池田満

Mononobe　物部

Naikū　内宮

Nan'ensho　南淵書

Nihon Shoki　日本書紀

Nobukata Kiyohara　清原宣賢

Norinaga Motoori　本居宣長

Ogasawara　小笠原

Ōtomo　大友

Rei Torii　鳥居禮

Reisō　霊宗

Ryukyu Shintōki　琉球神道記

Sadashizu Yoda　依田貞鎮

Saigen　斎元

Satsuki Narasaki　楢崎皐月

Seiji Takabatake　高畠精二

Seizō Kōno　河野省三

Sendai Kuji Hongi　先代旧事本紀

Sendai Kuji Hongi Taiseikyō　先代旧事本紀大成経

Shaku Nihongi　釈日本紀

Shiichi Kubota　窪田志一

Shin'ichi Hoshi　新一星

Shinden Jōdai Tennōki　神伝上代天皇紀

Shinto　神道

Shōtoku　聖徳太子

Sōgen　宗源

Tadahiro Aizawa　相沢忠洋

Takamagahara　高天原

Takenouchi　竹内

Tenpenchii　天変地異

Tsugaru Soto Sangunshi　東日流外三郡誌

Uetsufumi　上記

Uneme Nagano　長野采女

Urabe　卜部

Utsukushi-no-Mori Jinji　美社神字

Wado Kōsaka　高坂和導

Wakabayashi-ke Koki　若林家古記

Xi Wangmu　西王母

Xu Fu　徐福

Yamatai　邪馬台

Yamato　大和

Yasukazu Fuse　布施泰和

Yasutoshi Waniko   和仁估安聡

Yatabe no Kinmochi   矢田部公望

Yayoi   弥生

Yoshikaze Kira   吉良義風

Yoshinosuke Matsumoto   松本善之助

Yoshio Yamada   山田孝雄

Yoshizō Munakata   宗像良蔵

Yukikazu Yoshimi   吉見幸和

Yūnoshin Ibo   井保勇之進

Zankō Masuho   増穂残口

Bibliography

Akiyoneto. *Nazo no Katakamuna Bunmei*. Tokyo: Tokuma Shoten, 1981.

Akutsu, Jun. "Kagaku to Chokkan—Narasaki Satsuki no Katakamuna Kenkyū ni Miru Gen-Nihonjin-Zō." *Rekishi Dokuhon* "Koshi-Koden no Nazo." Tokyo: Shinjinbutsuōraisha, 1996.

Aston, William George. *Nihongi*. London: Japan Society, 1896.

Barber, Elizabeth Wayland and Paul T. Barber. *When They Severed Earth from Sky*. Princeton, N.J.: Princeton University Press, 2006.

Bentley, John R. *The Authenticity of Sendai Kuji Hongi: A New Examination of Texts, with a Translation and Commentary*. Boston: Brill, 2006.

Bialock, David. *Eccentric Spaces, Hidden Histories*. Palo Alto, Calif.: Stanford University Press, 2007.

Cayce, Edgar E., et al. *Mysteries of Atlantis Revisited*. New York: Harper & Row, 1988. Quoted in Peter R. Farley, *Where Were You Before the Tree of Life? Volume 1:* 116, www.4truthseekers.org/volume1_wwybttol.pdf. (I don't know how the author of this book learned about the Takenouchi Documents.)

Chouon, Dōkai. *Shigetsu Yawa* (1670). Quoted in *Nihon no Gisho* by Akira Fujiwara, 155–56. Tokyo: Bungei Shunjū, 2004.

Churchward, James. *The Books of the Golden Age*. Brotherhood of Life, 1997.

Corbin, Henry. *History of Islamic Philosophy*. London: Kegan Paul International, 1993.

Ehrman, Bart D. *Forged: Writing in the Name of God*. New York: HarperOne, 2011.

Ende, Michael, Erhard Eppler, and Hanne Tächl. *Oriibu no Mori de Katariau.* Tokyo: Iwanaga Shoten, 1984.

Evola, Julius. *Revolt Against the Modern World.* Rochester, Vt.: Inner Traditions, 1995.

———. *Meditations on the Peaks.* Rochester, Vt.: Inner Traditions, 1998.

———. *Men Among the Ruins: Post-War Reflections of a Radical Traditionalist.* Rochester, Vt.: Inner Traditions, 2002.

———. "Il barone sanguinario." Roma, February 9, 1973. Translated by Greg Johnson at www.counter-currents.com/2011/02/baron-von-ungern-sternberg.

Fitzgerald, Timothy. "Religion is not a standalone category." *The Immanent Frame,* October 29, 2008. http://blogs.ssrc.org/tif/2008/10/29/religion-is-not-a-standalone-category.

Fujiwara, Akira. *Nihon no Gisho.* Tokyo: Bungei Shunjū, 2004.

———. "Chūyo Nihongi to 'Koshi-Koden.'" *Rekishi Dokuhon* "'Koshi-koden' to 'Gisho' no Nazo wo Yomu." Tokyo: Shinjinbutsuōraisha (2012): 159.

———. "Kindai no Gisho: 'Chōkodaishi' kara 'Kindai Gisen Kokushi' e," *Gibunshogaku Nyūmon.* Edited by Toshihiko Hisano and Tsutomu Tokieda. Tokyo: Kashiwa Shoten, 2004.

Fukano, Kazuyuki. *Chōkagakusho "Katakamuna" no Nazo.* Tokyo: Kosaido Books, 1993.

Funai, Yukio. *Iyashirochi.* Tokyo: Hyogensha, 2004.

Fuse, Yasukazu. *'Takenouchi Monjo' no Nazo wo Toku.* Tokyo: Seiko Shobo, 2003.

———. *'Takenouchi Monjo' no Nazo wo Toku 2.* Tokyo: Seiko Shobo, 2011.

Godwin, Joscelyn. *Atlantis and the Cycles of Time.* Rochester, Vt.: Inner Traditions, 2010.

Goodman, David G. *Jews in the Japanese Mind: The History and Uses of a Cultural Stereotype.* Lexington Books, 2000.

Gotō, Takashi. *Sakitsumiyo no Furukoto no Mototsufumi Ōinaru Oshie.* Tokyo: Tokuma Shoten, 2004.

Gotō, Yoshihiro. "Kekarechi wo Iyashirochi ni suru Hōhō: Sono 7." *Nōgyō Keieisha,* February 2006.

Guénon, René. *Crisis of the Modern World*. Hillsdale, N.Y.: Sophia Perennis, 2001.

————. *Man and His Becoming according to the Vedānta*. Hillsdale, N.Y.: Sophia Perennis, 2004.

————. *The Essential René Guénon: Metaphysics, Tradition, and the Crisis of Modernity*. Bloomington, Ind.: World Wisdom, 2009.

————. *The King of the World*. Hillsdale, N.Y.: Sophia Perennis, 2001.

————. *The Reign of Quantity and the Signs of the Times*. Hillsdale, N.Y.: Sophia Perennis, 2004.

————. *Traditional Forms & Cosmic Cycles*. Hillsdale, N.Y.: Sophia Perennis, 2001.

Harada, Minoru. "Mō Hitotsu no 'Sendai Kuji Hongi'?" In Kisho *"Sendai Kuji Hongi" no Nazo wo Saguru*, edited by Biten Yasumoto, 348–372. Tokyo: Hihyōsha, 2007.

————. *Gensō no Kodai ōchō*. Tokyo: Hinansha, 1998. And e-mail communication with Matt Treyvaud.

————. "Kisho 'Takeuchi Monjo' Dan'atsu to 2.26 Jiken no Himerareta Kōsa." In *Rekishi wo Kaeta Gisho*. Tokyo: Japan Mix, 1996.

————. "Kojima *Kojiki*." In *Rekishi Dokuhon* "'Koshi-Koden' to 'Gisho' no Nazo wo Yomu" 2012.

————. *"Koshi-Koden" Itan no Kamigami*. Tokyo: Being Net Press, 2006.

————. "Koshi-koden Jiten." In *Rekishi Dokuhon* "Koshi-koden no Nazo," 1996.

————. *Nihon Tondemo Jinbutsu-den*. Autobiography of wartime engineer Ukichirō Nakaya, quoted, 189. Tokyo: Bungeisha, 2009.

Havens, Thomas R. H. *Farm and Nation in Modern Japan: Agrarian Nationalism, 1870–1940*. Princeton, N.J.: Princeton University Press, 1974.

Hideki, Saitō. "Sendai kuji hongi no gensetsu to seisei: hensei suru kodai shinwa ron to tame ni," *Kodai bungaku* 37 (March 1998). Quoted in *Eccentric Spaces, Hidden Histories* by David Bialock, 153. Palo Alto, Calif.: Stanford University Press, 2007.

Hisano, Toshihiko and Tsutomu Tokieda, eds. *Gibunshogaku Nyūmon*. Tokyo: Kashiwa Shoten, 2004.

Hitsuki Shinji. Ki no Maki 13:270. As quoted on the blog http://teru
.under.jp.

Ikeda, Mitsuru. *The World of the Hotsuma Legends*. Translated by Andrew
Driver. Tokyo: Japan Translation Center, 1996.

———. *Hotsuma Tsutaye wo Yomitoku*. Tokyo: Tenbōsha, 2001.

———. *Hotsuma Jōmon Nihon no Takara*. Tokyo: Tenbōsha, 2005.

Imura, Kōji. "Arafuka Michinari no Yūshiizen Kenkyū e no
Chōshinrigakuteki Approach." In *Rekishi Dokuhon* "Koshi-Koden no
Nazo." 66–79. Tokyo: Shinjinbutsuōraisha, 1996.

Inoue, Nobutaka, ed. "Sano Tsunehiko and 'Divine Principle (Shinri),'"
Contemporary Papers on Japanese Religion IV: Kami. Tokyo:
Kokugakuin University, 1998.

Ishida, Ittei. *Shōtoku Taishi Go Kenpō Shakugi*. Manuscript copy by Shinzō
Nakashima, 1978. Saga Prefectural Library. Saga: Japan.

Isomae, Jun'ichi. *Kindai Nihon no Shuukyou Gensetsu to Sono Keifu*. Tokyo:
Iwanami Soten, 2003.

Iwada, Sadao. "Kōtai Jingū Betsugū Izawa-no-miya Bōkei Jiken no Shinsō."
Kokugakuin Daigaku Nihon Bunka Kenkyūjo Kiyō 33 (1974): 1–100.

Jowett, Benjamin, trans. and ed. *The Dialogues of Plato*. Oxford: Clarendon
Press, 1953.

Kanō, Kōkichi. "Amatsukyō Kobunsho no Hihan." In *Rekishi Dokuhon*
"Koshi-Koden no Nazo," 347–73. Tokyo: Shinjinbutsuōraisha, 1996.
Originally published in Shisō, June 1936.

Kiku, Yamane. *Kirisuto ha Nihon de Shindeiru*. Tokyo: Tama Shuppan, 1975.

Kiyosuke, Michio. "'*Hotsuma Tsutaye*' Gishosetsu wo Koete." In *Rekishi
Dokuhon* "Kiken na Rekishisho 'Koshikoden,'" 179–87. Tokyo:
Shinjinbutsuōraisha, 2000.

Kołakowski, Leszek. *Modernity on Endless Trial*. Chicago, Ill.: University
of Chicago Press, 1990.

Kōno, Seizō. *Kuji-Taiseikyo ni kan suru Kenkyuu*. Tokyo: Geiensha, 1952.

Kōsaka, Wado. *Takenouchi Documents I*. Translation at http://takenouchi-
documents.com.

———. *Takenouchi Documents II*. Translation at http://takenouchi-
documents.com.

———. *Takenouchi Documents III.* Translation at http://takenouchi-documents.com.

———. *Chōzukai Takeuchi Monjo.* Tokyo: Tokuma Shoten, 1995.

Kume, Masafumi. *Sakai Katsutoki: "Itan" no Dentōsha.* Tokyo: Gakken Publishing, 2012.

Maier, Hans. *Totalitarianism and Political Religions,* Vol. 1. New York: Routledge, 2004.

Marrou, Henri-Irénée. *De la connaissance historique.* Paris: Editions du Seuil, 1954.

Masaki, Jinzaburō (Diary of, vol. 2). Tokyo: Yamagawa Shuppansha, 1981.

Matsumoto, Yoshinosuke. *The Hotsuma Legends: Paths of the Ancestors.* Translated by Andrew Driver. Tokyo: Japan Translation Center, 1999.

———. *Himerareta Nihon Kodaishi*  [*Hotsuma Tsutaye*]. Tokyo: Mainichi Shinbun, 1980.

———.  [*Hotsuma Tsutaye*]. Tōkyō: Hotsuma Kankōkai, 1993.

McGilchrist, Iain. *The Master and His Emissary.* New Haven, Conn.: Yale University Press, 2009.

Michel, John. *The Earth Spirit, Its Ways, Shrines and Mysteries.* London: Thames and Hudson, 1975.

Miyatō, Naoomi. *Shōtoku Taishi ni Erabu 17 Jō 5 Kenpō.* Tokyo: Bun-Ichi Sōgō Shuppan, 1995.

Morrow, Avery. "Patriotism, Secularism, and State Shintō: D. C. Holtom's Representations of Japan." *Wittenberg University East Asian Studies Journal* 36 (2011): 2–29.

Nagaki, Teiichi. "Kirisuto ha Naze Nihon ni Kita ka?" Tō-A Bunka Kyōkai, 1940. Quoted in Jyunku, "Amatsukyō to Yasue Norihiro," *Jinbōchō Wotawota Nikki.* August 27, 2011: http://d.hatena.ne.jp/jyunku/20110827/p1.

Nagaike, Tōru. 21 *seiki no Butsurigaku: Senshō Energy—Kūkan-ron.* Tokyo: Kyou no Wadai-sha, 2012.

Nagayama, Yasuo. *Gishi Bōken Sekai.* Tokyo: Chikuma Shobo, 2001.

Nakaya, Shin'ichi. "Shōtoku Taishi to Itan Bunsho 'Kuji Hongi' no Nazo." *Mu,* July 2013.

Nakazono, Mikoto Masahilo. *The Source of the Present Civilization.* Santa Fe, N.Mex.: Kototama Books, 1990.

Nasr, Seyyed Hossein. "Reply to Zailan Moris," in *The Philosophy of Seyyed Hossein Nasr.* As quoted in Algis Uždavinys, *The Golden Chain: An Anthology of Pythagorean and Platonic Philosophy.* World Wisdom, 2004.

Norinaga, Motoori. *Motoori Norinaga's The Two Shrines of Ise: An Essay of Split Bamboo.* Translated by Mark Teeuwen. Wiesbaden: Harrassowitz Verlag, 1995.

Nozawa, Tadanao. *Kinsho Shotōku Taishi Go Kenpō.* Tokyo: Shinjinbutsuōraisha, 2004.

Ofuka, Koyō and Ayumu Yasutomi. "Manshū no Byōe." *Ajia Keizai* 45, no. 5 (May 2004): 58–90.

Ogasawara, Haruo. Preface to *Zoku Shintō Taikei: Sendai Kuji Hongi Taiseikyō I.* Tokyo: Shintō Taikei Hensankai, 1999. Quoted in *Rekishi Dokuhon* "'Koshi-koden' to 'Gisho' no Nazo wo Yomu." Tokyo: Shinjinbutsuōraisha, 2012.

Okada, Mitsuhiro. "Koshi-koden to UFO." In *Rekishi Dokuhon* "Kiken na Rekishisho 'Koshi-Koden,'" 108–13. Tokyo: Shinjinbutsuōraisha, 2000.

Ooms, Herman. *Imperial Politics and Symbolics in Ancient Japan.* Honolulu: University of Hawai'i Press, 2009.

Philippi, Donald L. trans. *Kojiki.* Tokyo: University of Tokyo Press, 1968.

Plato. *Phaedrus.* Translated by Benjamin Jowett.

Reader, Ian. *Religious Violence in Contemporary Japan: The Case of Aum Shinrikyō.* Honolulu: University of Hawai'i Press, 2000.

Rekishi Dokuhon. "Koshi-Koden no Nazo." Tokyo: Shinjinbutsuōraisha, 1996.

———. "Kiken na Rekishisho 'Koshi-Koden.'" Tokyo: Shinjinbutsuōraisha, 2000.

———. "'Koshi-Koden' to 'Gisho' no Nazo wo Yomu." Tokyo: Shinjinbutsuōraisha, 2012.

———. "Koshi-Koden Catalog," "Kiken na Rekishisho 'Koshi-Koden.'" 2000.

Saitō, Ryuuichi. "'Kukami Bunken' ha 'Koden' de ha nai." In *Rekishi Dokuhon* "Koshi-Koden no Nazo," 1996.

Sakai, Katsutoki. 카미ⅠⅠ노아FLㅏ시 [*Kamiyo no Hanashi*] or *Jindai Hishi Hyakuwa*. Tokyo: Kokkyō Senmeidan, 1930.

———. "The Three Elements of Music." *Music* 15, no. 4 (February 1899).

———. *Sekai no Shōtai to Yudaya-jin*. Tokyo: Naigai Shobo, 1924. Quoted in Kume, *Sakai Katsutoki: "Itan" no Dentōsha*. Tokyo: Gakken Publishing, 2012.

Scheid, Bernhard. "Reading the *Yuiitsu shintō myōbō yōshū*: A Modern Exegesis of an Esoteric Shinto Text." In *Shinto in History: Ways of the Kami,* edited by John Breen and Mark Teeuwen, 117–43. Honolulu: University of Hawai'i Press, 2000.

Sekigawa, Jirō. *Katakamuna e no Michi*. Tokyo: Eco-Creative, 2009.

Senrei. *Nagano Uneme Den* (c. 1700). Quoted in Seizō Kōno, *Kuji-Taiseikyō ni kan suru Kenkyū*. Tokyo: Geiensha, 1952. Referenced in Haruo Ogasawara, "Gisho 'Taiseikyo' Shuppan no Hamon," *Rekishi wo Kaeta Gisho,* 113. Tokyo: Japan Mix, 1996.

Shillony, Ben-Ami, ed. *The Emperors of Modern Japan*. Boston: Brill Academic Publishing, 2008.

Shintō Taikei Hensankai, ed. *Zoku Shintō Taikei: Sendai Kuji Hongi Taiseikyō III*. Tokyo: Shintō Taikei Hensankai, 1999.

Suzumu, Shimazono. "State Shinto and Emperor Veneration." In *The Emperors of Modern Japan,* edited by Ben-Ami Shillony, 61–62. Brill Academic Publishing, 2008.

Tadashii Kyōiku wo Mamoru Kai. *Nihon no Jōkodai Bunka*. Tokyo: CMC, 2007.

Takahashi, Katsuhiko. "Mohaya Boku no Karada ya Monogatari no Ichibu de ari Ketsuniku to Natteirun Desu." In *Rekishi Dokuhon* "Kiken na Rekishisho 'Koshi-Koden,'" 2000.

Takeuchi, Mutsuhiro. "Mō hitotsu no 'Takeuchi Bunsho.'" In *Rekishi Dokuhon* "Koshi-Koden no Nazo," 82-91. Tokyo: Shinjinbutsuōraisha, 1996.

Tanaka, Katsuya. *Gishokō: uzumoreta kisho "Uetsufumi" no nazo*. Tokyo: Tōgensha, 1980.

Tanaka, Satoshi. "Mononobe Bunsho." In *Rekishi Dokuhon* "'Koshi-Koden' to 'Gisho' no Nazo wo Yomu," 2012.

Teeuwen, Mark. "Sendai Kuji Hongi: Authentic Myths or Forged History?" *Monumenta Nipponica* no. 62.1 (2007): 87–96.

Tolkien, J. R. R. *The Tolkien Reader.* New York: Ballantine, 1966.

Torii, Rei. *Amaterasu Ōmikami Danshinron.* Tokyo: Forest Shuppan, 2002.

———. *Hotsuma Monogatari.* Tokyo: Shinsensha, 2005.

———. *Nihon Chōkodaishi ga Akasu Kamigami no Nazo.* Tokyo: Nihon Bungeisha, 1997.

Tsushima, Michihito. "Emperor and World Renewal in the New Religions: The Case of Shinsei Ryūjinkai." In *New Religions.* Tokyo: Kokugakuin Institute for Japanese Culture and Classics, 1991. www2.kokugakuin.ac.jp/ijcc/wp/cpjr/newreligions/tsushima.html.

Tsushima, Michihito, ed. *Shinsei Ryūjin Kai: Himitsu Shinji Shiryō Shūhei.* Tokyo: Hachiman Press, 1994. Quoted in Masafumi Kume, *Sakai Katsutoki: "Itan" no Dentōsha.* Tokyo: Gakken Publishing, 2012: 491.

"Ushinawareta MU Taiheiyōjō Himitsu no Tobira wo Aku," *Sunday Mainichi,* August 7, 1932. Quoted in Naho Fujiho, "Gisho to yabō no kanbotsu tairiku: Mū tairiku no denpa to Nihon-teki juyō," In *Rekishi wo Kaeta Gisho,* 64, 69. Tokyo: Japan Mix (1996).

Uždavinys, Algis. *The Golden Chain: An Anthology of Pythagorean and Platonic Philosophy.* Bloomington, Ind.: World Wisdom, 2004.

Yoda, Sadashizu. *Hen Mui Shinpi Shoden.* Tatsu-59, Iwase Bunko Library, microfilm frame 77. Iwase City, Aichi, Japan.

Yuasa, Yoshiko. "Masuho Zankō—Sendai Kuji Hongi Taiseikyō." *Tōkyō Gakugei Daigaku Kiyō Jinbunkagaku* 48 (1997): 315–23.

Index